Civil Procedure, Culture, and Proportionality

Gustavo Osna

Civil Procedure, Culture, and Proportionality

Springer

Gustavo Osna
Universidade Federal do Paraná
Curitiba, Paraná, Brazil

ISBN 978-3-032-27554-7 ISBN 978-3-032-27555-4 (eBook)
https://doi.org/10.1007/978-3-032-27555-4

Translation from the Portuguese language edition: "Processo Civil, Cultura e Proporcionalidade" by Gustavo Osna, © Author 2017. Published by Thomson Reuters. All Rights Reserved.

The original submitted manuscript has been translated into English. The translation was done using artificial intelligence. A subsequent revision was performed by the author(s) to further refine the work and to ensure that the translation is appropriate concerning content and scientific correctness. It may, however, read stylistically different from a conventional translation.

This Springer imprint is published by the registered company Springer Nature Switzerland AG
The registered company address is: Gewerbestrasse 11, 6330 Cham, Switzerland

Competing Interests The author has no competing interests to declare that are relevant to the content of this manuscript.

Contents

1 **Introduction** ... 1

2 **Civil Procedure as a Dynamic Reality** ... 3
2.1 Law, the Liberal State, and the Jurisdictional Monopoly ... 3
2.2 The Change in Values and Its Impact on the Proceedings ... 10
2.3 Civil Procedure: Means and Ends ... 15
References ... 18

3 **Why Critically Analyze Civil Procedure?** ... 21
3.1 Civil Procedure as a Cultural Issue ... 21
3.2 The Judicial Process: Concepts and Rituals ... 29
3.3 Reasons to Question the Judicial Process ... 36
References ... 39

4 **How to Critically Analyze Civil Procedure?** ... 41
4.1 The Real Limits of Civil Procedure ... 41
4.2 The Democratic Barriers of Civil Procedure ... 48
4.3 Civil Procedure as a Framework of Institutional Choices ... 52
References ... 55

5 **Critically Reconstructing Civil Procedure** ... 57
5.1 Bringing Elements Together: Proportionality and Civil Procedure ... 57
5.2 Proportionality and Civil Procedure in Comparative Perspective ... 63
5.3 Conceptual Keys and Proportionality ... 69
References ... 76

6 **Reimagining Civil Procedure: Possibilities and Alternatives** ... 79
6.1 Alternative Dispute Resolution Methods ... 79
6.2 Collective Proceedings and Procedural Management ... 87
6.3 Compositional Process: Structural Decisions and Social Impact ... 95
References ... 100

7 Final Considerations 103

References 105

Chapter 1
Introduction

> Due process requires that procedures be fair, but fairness is a pragmatic ideal. It provides protection to the individual, but not in a manner that would necessitate the sacrifice of other important rights.

The above sentence was authored by Owen Fiss. Through it, the reader can grasp one of the most sensitive challenges of contemporary civil procedure: its articulation with the possibilities and needs of material reality.

This challenge, though indispensable, is to some extent new to continental civil procedure. This is because, traditionally, procedural law has been understood from a purely theoretical perspective. The main concerns were related to its academic and doctrinal discourse, with little attention paid to its conditions of verification. As a result, books could become detached from reality.

However, the gap between the two worlds (theory and practice) has at times become an abyss, and the need for rapprochement has become increasingly evident. Otherwise, theoretical and normative promises may simply fail to materialize in reality. The legal process and its guarantees risk becoming nothing more than a fairy tale for a large portion of the population.

Is it appropriate to speak of guarantees such as a "day in court" without considering the real possibilities of fulfilling this principle and its underlying purposes? Can the protection of "due process" occur without a cultural understanding of what constitutes "due process"?

This work seeks to offer the reader a distinctive approach to this type of issue. To this end, it adopts a somewhat unorthodox path in understanding civil procedure: viewing it as an inevitably cultural and contextual phenomenon. This perspective underscores its malleability and challenges some of the foundational dogmas upon which it is based.

To enable this construction, the first chapter is dedicated to providing a brief overview of the recent history of the continental process. In doing so, it presents some of the most relevant pillars of its formation, as well as its main challenges and paradoxes.

G. Osna, *Civil Procedure, Culture, and Proportionality*,
https://doi.org/10.1007/978-3-032-27555-4_1

Subsequently, in the second chapter, this background is used as a basis to argue for the necessity of understanding civil procedural law from a critical (or skeptical) perspective. Its cultural and contextual nature requires that, within its scope, there must be an important place reserved for doubt and uncertainty, which, provided legitimacy is maintained, allows for its deconstruction.

In the third chapter, the premises established allow for the construction of an objective line of reasoning: as a cultural and flexible phenomenon, the civil procedure is composed of choices. Along these lines, real limitations (such as costs and technical complexity) are also presented, which cause this creative construction to encounter constant barriers, requiring sacrifices and curbing utopian discourse.

All of this confirms that the "castle" of procedure is, in fact, an architectural project in constant revision. The last two chapters are devoted precisely to this forward-looking exercise. In the fourth chapter, we describe how the criterion of proportionality, in its broad sense, can play a significant role in reinterpreting procedure (by articulating the cultural, normative, and structural elements underlying its operation). In the fifth chapter, we point out some concrete procedural impacts that result from this approach, as well as avenues for its further exploration.

With this comprehensive approach, the aim is to provide the reader with both support for understanding the current state of the continental procedure and possible guidelines for its improvement. The most important objective is to offer resources for a more effective process, enhancing the quality of judicial services. The goal is to bridge theory and practice, allowing them to advance together.

Chapter 2
Civil Procedure as a Dynamic Reality

2.1 Law, the Liberal State, and the Jurisdictional Monopoly

It is common in academic circles to emphasize the significance of liberal influence on the development of continental legal thought. As we move through fields such as constitutional law and civil procedure, we observe that this focus becomes even more prevalent. Topics such as the "French Revolution" and the "Enlightenment mentality" are frequently brought to the fore, with considerable attention devoted to their discussion.

This appeal does not appear to us to be unfounded. On the contrary, its significance is evident, providing a fundamental basis for understanding why our legal framework has its current contours.[1] Even though there is a risk of repetition, the inquiry is relevant to ensure that our institutions are better understood.

However, we consider that a generic reference to the "essence" or "liberal roots" of our system is insufficient. Taking a step further, it is necessary to address the

[1] "The Liberal Rule of Law, faced with the need to curb the abuses of the preceding regime, established the principle of legality as the foundation for its imposition. This principle elevated the law to a supreme act, aiming to eliminate the legal traditions of absolutism and the *ancien régime*. From that point on, the administration and the judiciary were prevented from invoking any right or public interest that conflicted with the law." Furthermore, it is asserted that "the principle of legality thus became a criterion for identifying the law; the law would exist solely in the legal norm, whose validity would not depend on its correspondence with justice, but only on having been enacted by an authority vested with normative competence," and that "for the development of society amid freedom, there was an aspiration for a predictable law or the so-called 'legal certainty'—understood here as the guarantee of certainty of a prior and determined meaning attributed to the norm. The aim was for an abstract law, capable of encompassing any future concrete situations, thereby eliminating the need for the enactment of new laws (…) obviously, a law marked by generality and abstraction would be of no use if the judge could adapt it to different concrete situations. According to liberal values, this would undermine the predictability and certainty of the law, which were considered indispensable for the maintenance of freedom." See Marinoni (2005) and Marinoni et al. (2015a), pp. 29–34.

G. Osna, *Civil Procedure, Culture, and Proportionality*,
https://doi.org/10.1007/978-3-032-27555-4_2

consequences and impacts of this aspect, opening the door to some questions: What are the main characteristics of this "liberal mindset"? In what ways has it influenced the development of our legal thought? What are its most visible effects?

Without intending to exhaust the subject, we can illustrate in a didactic manner that the answer to these questions begins with several central elements: centralization, predictability, minimal nature, and individualism. From these perspectives, the changes introduced by this new structure, as well as its role in breaking with the previously existing model, become clearer.

In fact, in a brief analysis, it is no exaggeration to state that prior to the value changes our theorist labeled as "liberalism," the State bore little resemblance to what we know today. Instead of a structure characterized by a central and exclusive authority, the prevailing model was marked by social dispersion and the valorization of groups. The Liberal State moved in the opposite direction of this logic. By concentrating prerogatives, it sought to establish a polarized and exclusionary "public power."

In light of this, whereas previously the coexistence of numerous spheres of authority was tolerated, from this point onward, the legitimate use of force comes to be recognized as an exclusively state prerogative.[2] The very notion of the "subject" acquires new meaning: while the collective was previously foregrounded, the liberal ideal shifted the focus to the individual as such.[3] It is in the individual that the limit to state authority is found, thereby intensifying the dichotomy between "public" and "private."

In short, there was a shift from a model characterized by diffusion to a centralizing logic, impacting the structure of society. The promise of security played a decisive role in this process: on one hand, the formation of the state entity would

---

[2] According to Max Weber, "in the past, the most varied institutions—from the clan onward—regarded the use of physical force as perfectly normal. Today, however, we must say that the State is a human community that successfully claims the *monopoly on the legitimate use of physical force* within a given territory (...) specifically, at present, the right to use physical force is granted to other institutions or individuals only to the extent that the State permits it. The State is regarded as the sole source of the 'right' to use violence." In the same vein, Bobbio states that "medieval society was a pluralist society, as it was composed of a plurality of social groups, each possessing its own legal order: law there appeared as a social phenomenon, produced not by the State, but by civil society. With the formation of the modern State, by contrast, society assumes a monist structure, in the sense that the State concentrates all powers within itself, first and foremost the power to create law: it is not content to merely participate in this creation, but seeks to be the sole entity to establish law, either directly through legislation, or indirectly through the recognition and control of customary norms. Thus, we witness what in another course we have called the *process of monopolization of legal production by the State*." Weber (2002), p. 56. Bobbio (1995), p. 27.

[3] Hespanha states that "it came to be understood that those universal attributes or qualities ascribed to individuals (being *pater familias*, being a plebeian), which describe the social relations in which they are integrated, are not qualities incorporated into their essence (...) but are rather mere names, external to the essence, and can therefore be disregarded when considering that essence. If we do so, we obtain a series of 'naked' individuals, without distinguishing features, interchangeable, abstract, general, equal. True atoms of a society (...) Once society is forgotten, that is, the set of inter-individual bonds, what remains is the individual, detached, isolated." Hespanha (2005), p. 117.

result from an individual concession, with individuals relinquishing some of their powers in favor of the State itself. On the other hand, predictability would serve as the desired counterpart to this renunciation, underpinning the acceptance of a central authority.

- In a model with dispersed powers, there could be greater mistrust regarding the behavior of a given actor and their compliance with some external factor. The Rule of Law would emerge to reinforce this security, which is essential for social relations. For example, when a consumer provides their credit card information to make an online purchase or leaves their car with a valet service, it is because they intuitively trust in the conformity of the conduct to be adopted.

To a large extent, this was the central argument of the contractarian discourse.[4] It is through this circular movement between expectations and concessions, between promises and acknowledgments, that public authority would forge its domain. Consequently, it is also from this process that it should derive its characteristics and means of action.

This clarifies why it is commonly stated that the Liberal State had a minimal and neutral genesis. Essentially, these were the attributes that shaped its very structure. Contrary to what is common today, the notion of an active state, aimed at reducing inequalities or providing services such as health or education to the community, was not considered. At that time, the fundamental idea was different: a limited state, dedicated solely to protecting the individual freedom of each person and incapable of interfering with it.[5]

[4] "The thematization of sovereignty and law passes through the filter of a new philosophical anthropology: grasped in its essential and perennial traits, the individual is removed from the logic of belonging and connection with bodies to be represented as a unitary subject of necessity and rights, defined by the parameters of liberty and equality. The liberty of the subject is not, however, a form of lawlessness detached from any bond: it is, on the one hand, a space protected from undue intrusions by others (…); on the other hand, it is a relationship with the law, a possibility for action and personal expansion that finds in the law its foundation, its limit, its guarantee (…) the individual is free insofar as he acts within the bounds of the law, and the law, in turn, is the only instrument capable of protecting him from arbitrariness. It is precisely from the nexus between liberty and law that the possibility arises to contain the arbitrariness of the sovereign and to safeguard the security of subjects." Costa (2006), p. 102.

[5] "The transformations observed are not confined to the political sphere; they neither originate nor are exhausted solely within this domain. Liberal revolutions also have a social character, and with the fall of old governments, old habits are also overthrown, affecting classes, class strata, and their respective zones of influence or communication; some values are lost while others are acquired. A reorganization of power both drives and is driven by a new organization of society. Hence, the emphasis on the legal freedoms of the individual, such as freedom of contract; the absolutization of private property alongside these freedoms; the long-standing refusal to recognize freedom of association (based on the principle that association diminishes individual freedom and, in practice, out of fear of the strength of associations formed by the economically weaker); and deviations from democratic principles (despite their formal proclamation), notably through the restriction of voting rights to those possessing certain assets or income, as only those with social responsibilities should, it was argued, have political responsibilities (census suffrage)." Miranda (2003), p. 88.

For the same reasons, this detached and abstentionist stance also required the public authorities to adopt neutrality as a central standard. The issue can be easily summarized: since it is not the State's role to reorder society but merely to contain possible violations of each individual's freedom, there would be no theoretical justification for treating people differently. Any particularities would be disregarded, in line with the very emphasis on predictability and formal equality—"*seeing like a State*," in the words of James Scott.[6]

In summary, considering this caricature of the post-revolutionary State, we note that its values and its parameters of legitimacy were quite specific. It was from this framework (abstentionist, neutral, and exclusionary) that public action was to be assessed by investigating the effectiveness of its performance.[7]

At this point, however, a couple of questions may arise: What is the relationship between this series of aspects and Law? Why are they relevant to a work dedicated to civil procedure?

The response to these provocations can be stated simply: the legal system and the procedural model cannot be viewed as isolated entities. As identified by Daniel Mitidiero, the approach adopted for dispute resolution is in dialogue both with the state context and with the social environment in which it is embedded.[8] The interconnection between these aspects is not only necessary but also inevitable.

Thus, in understanding the characteristic framework of the Liberal State, it is necessary to recognize that the legal field was also shaped by its central tenets. In this regard, a first and most obvious example of this interaction stems from the inherently exclusionary and centralizing nature that defined the state itself. This is because, as liberal thought sought to eliminate the existence of parallel spheres of authority, it was only natural that it also attempted to monopolize the prerogative of regulating conduct. This paved the way for the transition from a pluralism of sources to state monism.[9] This was the path that led to "law" and "statute" being regarded as synonymous, seeking to confer legal validity solely on legislation enacted by the State.[10]

---

[6] Scott (1998).

[7] "If it is correct that, by the end of the nineteenth century, jurisdiction was fully aligned with the values of the Liberal State and legal positivism, what now becomes relevant is the relationship of these values, together with the conception of jurisdiction as a function aimed at enforcing violated private subjective rights. The proceduralists who defined this idea of jurisdiction were ideologically influenced by the model of the Liberal Rule of Law, and therefore subject to the values of formal equality, individual liberty—through the non-interference of the State in private relations—and the principle of separation of powers as a mechanism for subordinating both the executive and the judiciary to the law." Marinoni et al. (2010), p. 11.

[8] "Civil procedural law, as an expression of culture, is evidently not immune to the influence of the characteristics that society imparts to the State (…) The formalism of procedure must adapt to the instruments through which the State seeks to achieve social objectives, ensuring the rule of law." Mitidiero (2011), p. 55.

[9] Hespanha (2012).

[10] "The State, enclosed in its insularity, engages only with the outside world and only with other similar state entities; internally, it merely dictates the conditions under which a rule emerges from

In summary, while at other times the coexistence of different spheres of authority and standards of behavioral regulation might have been acceptable, the *centralizing* shift that marked the formation of the Modern State reversed this logic. To this end, efforts were made to grant the public exclusive authority in the creation of Law. Although this is materially debatable, given the existence of social institutions[11] or social facts,[12] this reduction was an essential piece of the puzzle during that period.

Similarly, considering the core values of liberalism, it becomes clear why written legislation (general and predictable) was conceived as the central instrument for social organization. In addition to the prevailing belief that it represented the purest

---

the confused limbo of merely social norms and becomes a legal one (…) legal experience must conform to the models of conduct established by sovereign will; it must develop in an obsequiously legalistic direction, always *secundum eventum legem*. And for control to be perfect, the law must be general and rigid, but also clear and certain; and it must be written; written in a text accessible to every citizen; and it may be decreed (as indeed it is) that ignorance of its provisions does not exempt one from the obligation to comply. Modern statism, in short, translates for law and for jurists into a burdensome monism and perpetuates throughout modernity (…) a legal absolutism." Grossi (2005), p. 30.

[11] "Institutions are experienced as something endowed with external reality; in other words, the institution is something situated outside the individual, something that in a certain way (in quite a demanding way, we might say) differs from the reality formed by the individual's thoughts, feelings, and fantasies. By this characteristic, an institution resembles other entities of external reality, bearing a certain similarity even to objects such as trees, tables, and telephones, which are out there, whether the individual wishes it or not. The individual would not be able to eliminate a tree with a wave of the hand, nor an institution. Language is experienced in this way (…) Institutions are experienced as possessing objectivity. This statement merely repeats, in a somewhat different form, the previous proposition. Something is objectively real when everyone (or almost everyone) acknowledges that it in fact exists, and that it exists in a particular way. This latter aspect is very important. There is correct English and incorrect English—and this remains so, objectively so, even if the individual thinks that the rules governing the matter are the height of absurdity (…) Institutions are endowed with coercive power. To some extent, this quality is implicit in the two already mentioned: the essential power that the institution exerts over the individual consists precisely in the fact that it has objective existence and cannot be dismissed by the individual. However, if the individual fails to notice this fact, forgets it—or, worse still—wishes to change the existing state of affairs, it is at this point that the coercive power of the institution is likely to present itself in a rather harsh manner. In an enlightened middle-class family, and at an age when everyone agrees such lapses are to be expected, the child is generally subjected to gentle persuasion while violating the standards of correct English. This gentle persuasion may continue to be applied in a progressive school, but it will rarely be so by the peers the child encounters there. These will most likely react to any infraction of their code of correct English (which is evidently not the same as the teacher's) with brutal mockery." Berger and Berger (1977), pp. 195–197.

[12] According to Durkheim, "in every society there is a specific group of phenomena that are distinguished by defined characteristics from those studied by other natural sciences. When I perform my role as a brother, husband, or citizen, when I fulfill the commitments I have undertaken, I am carrying out duties that are defined outside myself and my actions, in law and in customs. Even if they are in accordance with my own feelings and I inwardly sense their reality, this does not make them any less objective (…) the system of signs I use to express my thoughts, the system of currency I use to pay my debts, the credit instruments I employ in my commercial relations, the practices observed in my profession, etc. (…) these types of conduct or thought are not only external to the individual, but are also endowed with an imperative and coercive force by virtue of which they impose themselves upon him, whether he wishes it or not." Durkheim (2007), pp. 1–2.

expression of democracy, it was also thought that, through general provisions, it would be possible to regulate social events in a predictable and egalitarian manner. The importance of the notion of legality was emphasized, establishing it as a limit to state action.[13]

In the same vein, this *minimal* design of the state apparatus also shaped the very structure of interests then recognized as rights. Thus, a system was established based on the protection of essentially negative and individual values,[14] with particular emphasis on the guarantee of property. The State was assigned a dual function: (i) to intervene whenever necessary to restrain other individuals who might disrupt such exercise; and (ii) to refrain, itself, from causing such disruption—finding in individual liberty the limit of its own action.[15]

- In summary, the central idea of the period was to confine Law to state legislation—regarded as democratic and neutral. The aim was to restrain potential arbitrariness and ensure formally equal treatment for all. For example, by establishing that coercion is grounds for the annulment of legal transactions, written legislation would (allegedly) guarantee that this rule applied to all parties. There should be no room for arbitrariness or discrimination related to this factor.

Turning to our central subject, we note that the emergence of a centralizing State was also decisive for the development of civil procedural law. Moreover, within the context of a liberal State, a procedural system was established that also bore distinctly liberal characteristics. This issue appears to be crucial, as it explains the very establishment of the jurisdictional monopoly.

---

[13] "The revolutionaries believed that Parliament would produce law through the work of the nation's representatives guided by reason; and because the law was, at once, a rule created by the nation through its representatives (a matter of form) and guided by reason (a matter of substance), it could not violate justice or liberty. The liberal veneration of law produced consequences. The veneration of law as both form and substance was, gradually, replaced by a mere veneration of law as form. The identification of law with statute ultimately gave rise to an entirely formalist conception of legal experience." Clève (1995), pp. 34–35.

[14] "Fundamental rights, at least as recognized in the earliest written Constitutions, are a peculiar product (with the exception of certain social elements characteristic of French constitutionalism) of eighteenth-century liberal-bourgeois thought. They are marked by a strongly individualistic character, conceived as rights of the individual vis-à-vis the State, more specifically as rights of defense, delineating a sphere of non-intervention by the State and an area of individual autonomy in relation to its power. For this reason, they are presented as 'negative' rights, since they require abstention rather than positive action on the part of public authorities, and are thus understood as 'rights of resistance or opposition to the State.'" Sarlet et al. (2012), p. 260.

[15] According to Orlando Gomes, "under the capitalist system, the unitary concept of property is restored and the powers it confers are, at first, exaggerated, with an emphasis on the individualist conception. Its exercise is subject to few, if any, restrictions, and the right of the owner is elevated to the status of a natural right, on equal footing with fundamental freedoms (…) in the liberal state, the contract became the foremost instrument of autonomy of will, which was equated with freedom itself—both unthinkable without the right to private property. Freedom of contract and freedom of property would be interdependent, like conjoined twins." Gomes (2010), p. 111.

Just as occurred with the legislative phenomenon, the attempt to concentrate authority in the hands of the State also led the public entity to seek to reserve exclusively for itself the prerogative of settling disputes and resolving conflicts by imposing its decision on both parties involved in the matter. In the words of Ovídio Baptista da Silva, "*[T]he overwhelming growth of the modern State is closely linked to the monopoly over the production and application of law, and therefore to the creation of law, whether at the legislative or the judicial level.*"[16]

Thus, to this day, there is little debate regarding the monopolistic nature of jurisdictional activity (conceived in its entirety[17]). The resolution of disputes has become an activity to be performed exclusively by the State—creating obstacles to private justice and imposing on the State the obligation to develop alternatives to address this prohibition.[18]

Delving deeper into the investigation, we consider that the procedures and the parameters established at that time for dispute resolution were also strongly influenced by the liberal mindset. Thus, it became common to rely on a classical notion of the "separation of powers" to argue that judges should not, under any circumstances, go beyond the literal meaning of the legal text.[19] Furthermore, structures

[16] See Silva (2000), p. 23.

[17] The term "total" understanding of jurisdiction is used here insofar as, as is well known, there has been a recurring debate regarding the possibility of attributing a jurisdictional nature to arbitration. In this sense, it is argued that, since arbitration also resolves disputes, this mechanism would likewise possess such a qualification. It is precisely for this reason that a broad definition of "jurisdiction" is warranted, establishing that, as used here, the concept refers to an activity necessarily vested with *imperium*—thus limiting it to the state sphere. In this regard, Talamini emphasizes that "although legitimate and fully compatible with the guarantee of inalienable judicial protection, arbitral activity is private. The arbitrator does not exercise state jurisdiction. Its origin lies in a contractual act between the parties—regulated, and even protected and encouraged by the State. But there is no act of state delegation. If the term 'jurisdiction' is to be used in its classical sense, as one of the forms of expression of the sovereign power of the State, arbitration is not 'jurisdictional.'" From this, he concludes that "a consequence of the non-state character of arbitration is that arbitrators do not possess state *imperium*. They cannot adopt coercive measures. Whenever such measures are needed, they must turn to the judicial authority." Talamini (2015), p. 288.

[18] "Once the State is organized and its legal order established—which entails the imposition of rules of conduct to be observed by citizens—citizens are automatically prohibited from defending or enforcing their own interests (self-help) when such interests are protected by objective law. In other words, we understand the prohibition of self-help as an indispensable prerequisite for the organization and very existence of the State. As a consequence of this prohibition, there also arises, as a prerequisite, the State's duty and authority to provide jurisdiction to all citizens, since they cannot resort to self-help." Silva and Gomes (2010), p. 83.

[19] Analyzing the Italian model, Pasquino states that there, "one of the central functions of the separation of the judiciary from the legislative and executive powers has always been to limit or prevent the arbitrary exercise of judicial power by the monarch, who already possessed the other two powers. The Old Regime practice of the *lettres de cachet*, by which the king arbitrarily imprisoned or deprived defenseless citizens of their rights, is well known (…) it was during the Enlightenment that the idea of the 'rule of law' became established in the culture of the European continent, prior to its introduction into positive law during the French Revolution. Rule of law here means, in Lockean terms, government by public, stable, general, and abstract norms (…) a judiciary, separated from the legislature, in an institutional system that distinguishes both the organs exercising

were developed in which there was a prevailing disregard for the specific circumstances of the dispute, such as the urgency of relief or the need for preventive and specific interventions.[20] A generalist process was established, guided especially and essentially by values such as predictability and formal equality.[21]

- In a procedural model based on liberal values, the main objective would be to ensure that the same process applies to any party. For example, even if someone required immediate injunctive relief or an atypical specific remedy, or if the time allowed for a defense was significantly shortened, given the complexity of the case, there should be no room for judicial modification. The path would be singular and unavoidable.

2.2 The Change in Values and Its Impact on the Proceedings

It has been shown so far that the development of the continental legal process was strongly influenced by the values characteristic of the Liberal State, shaping the structures designed for dispute resolution. Thus, in an ongoing dialogue, civil procedure also incorporated this axiology at the core of its central framework.

---

these two functions and the functions themselves, is, in its autonomy, according to Montesquieu's literal phrasing, a *null* power. The judges act as nothing more than the 'bouche de la loi.'" Pasquino (2001), p. 210.

[20] "A judgment that has become res judicata is indisputable and enforceable (...) but as enforceable, the judgment offers the litigant a much broader range of possibilities than in the previous aspect. Enforcement allows something that, until the moment of res judicata, was legally impossible: the invasion of another's individual sphere and its material transformation to satisfy the interests of the party declared victorious in the judgment. It is no longer a matter of obtaining something with the cooperation of the adversary, but precisely against their will." Couture (1942), pp. 273–274.

[21] According to Marinoni, Arenhart, and Mitidiero, "the requirement to provide uniform treatment to social positions and rights is a characteristic imposition of the era of the classical liberal State, which was concerned with guaranteeing the freedom and rights of the bourgeois class. It was assumed that, in order to preserve freedom intact, the State could not provide differentiated treatment to individuals and rights (...) the need to safeguard freedom led to the affirmation of *formal* equality, resulting in the abstraction of differences between individuals and property (...) if formal equality inspires the legal system, presenting itself as a prerequisite for ensuring freedom and the proper functioning of the market, it is not possible to conceive of judicial protection that takes into account certain socially relevant interests or a form of 'differentiated judicial protection' that would reveal the need to grant 'differentiated treatment' to distinct situations and social positions." From this, they conclude that "as is clear, the drafting of the Codes of Civil Procedure of 1939 and 1973 was not only influenced by, but expressly admitted the 'purpose of instituting a single type for actions.' According to the 1973 Explanatory Memorandum, this purpose was in line with the 'modern principles of procedural science,' which emerged at the end of the nineteenth century and was consolidated through the systematic or Chiovendian school." See Marinoni et al. (2015b), pp. 25 and 33.

It should be noted that, in a brief overview, this identity has been profoundly shaken over the past century. Factors, such as changes in economic parameters,[22] the intangibility of post-war effects,[23] and the loss of faith in the rule of law, have led to fundamental changes in the sociocultural context.[24]

Examining this transformation more closely, we observe that the transition from a predominantly liberal State to a model more oriented toward welfare involved significant reallocations within the public sector, requiring a comprehensive reassessment of its role. Similarly, the field of Economics also underwent profound changes, notably with the rise of Keynesian ideals.[25] Although this analysis has

---

[22] After all, as recognized by Ripert, there is a dialogical relationship between the reproduction of the mode of production and the configuration of the state entity. In the author's words, "one cannot understand the evolution of our civil legislation over the past century and a half without taking into account the form of the economy. Laws are peace treaties between forces, continuously examined and revised. It is easy to recognize which victorious force each of these laws imposed. Industrial and financial capitalism created legislation that allowed it to assert its power (...) It is said that capitalism is liberal because it was born under the sign of liberty and considered freedom a useful means for its survival. But if it had to be content with common law, it could not have developed. Freedom was not enough for it." Ripert (1947), pp. 14–22.

[23] "Until then, war was a marginal activity, of interest to certain social groups by tradition or profession, and could develop in parallel with other national activities. From 1914 onward, war became a totalitarian social phenomenon, subordinating all tasks and occupations to its purposes, directly involving all social classes without exception (...) The Great War of 1914-1918 put an end to this romantic conception of military activity: since then, nothing has escaped the absolutism of war—economy, science, art, and even religion (...) Reproducing the phenomenon observed after the First World War, contemporary law, far from eliminating the normative provisions of economic content arising from the needs of war, tends instead to transform and systematize them (...)." Comparato (1965), pp. 15–17.

[24] Norberto Bobbio emphasizes that "it was from the critique of egalitarian doctrines against the conception and liberal practice of the State that the demands for social rights emerged, profoundly transforming the system of relations between the individual and the State and the very organization of the State, even in regimes that consider themselves to be continuators, without abrupt changes, of the nineteenth-century liberal tradition (...) Liberalism and egalitarianism are rooted in profoundly different conceptions of society: individualist, conflictual, and pluralist in the case of liberalism; totalizing, harmonious, and monist in the case of egalitarianism. For the liberal, the main purpose is the expansion of individual personality, abstractly considered as a value in itself; for the egalitarian, this purpose is the harmonious development of the community. The ways of conceiving the nature and tasks of the State are also different: limited and guarantor, the liberal State; interventionist and dirigiste, the egalitarian State." And this transformative logic is not concluded. On the contrary, there is room for the subsequent recognition of aspects such as constitutional centrality and its impacts on State action (leading to what has come to be known as the "Constitutional State"). See Bobbio (2000), p. 42.

[25] "John Maynard Keynes had been an early critic of the disastrous, bungled effort to restore a global economic order after World War I. In his prescient 1920 book, *The Economic Consequences of the Peace*, he inveighed against both the attempt to reestablish the prewar gold standard and the draconian reparations extracted from defeated Germany. The worsening instability of the global economy during the 1920s vindicated his criticism, and by the time of the cataclysmic world depression, the mature Keynes was fashioning his insights into his magisterial *General Theory* (...) for Keynes, the international realm of the laissez-faire economy displayed a special version of his general theory, especially vulnerable to instability and depression and resistant to stabilization.

faced various criticisms, particularly regarding the high, inseparable costs associated with its model,[26] it is clear that this, too, marked a turning point.

This is how the values described in the previous section became the subject of questioning, marking a trajectory characterized by dissent.[27] Whereas previously ideas such as the restriction and neutrality of the public sphere prevailed, it has become common to argue that the State should also be assigned other functions. Through movements that are not always convergent, new filters of legitimacy (such as "efficiency" or "participatory democracy") have come to be proposed for the State, requiring structural and institutional rearrangements.[28]

Given this, since the coupling between state action and the legal sphere has become historically insurmountable, it would be natural for the legal domain to also undergo the consequences of this transformation. Thus, the more active role of the State was normatively framed in texts such as the Mexican Constitution of 1917 and

---

An individual nation, with a relatively self-sufficient national economy (…) could manipulate total demand to generate adequate rates of savings, investment growth, and employment. But an open global economy of cross-national trade (…) tended to intensify periodic depressions." Kuttner (1992), pp. 26–27. Presenting Keynes's theoretical framework, see, among others, Keynes (1936).

[26] "In the social rule of law, profound symptoms of crisis can be observed—the so-called crisis of the welfare state, stemming not so much from ideological causes (the retreat of socialist or socializing ideas in the face of neoliberal ones) as from financial causes (the unbearable costs of increasingly extensive services for ever smaller active populations), administrative causes (the burden of bureaucracy, often accompanied by corruption), and commercial causes (the loss of competitiveness, in a globalizing economy, to countries without the same level of social protection)." Miranda (2003), p. 100.

[27] "During the nineteenth century, it was easy to look to the idea of a Constitution to define the political system, since, being consistent in its regulation and respected, a State that had a Constitution qualified as a constitutional State. In the twentieth century, everything changed: forms were accepted without adherence to principles, compromises were made between forces that could not neutralize each other, the same principles acquired different meanings, and, when inscribed in legal texts, they did not always succeed in securing the agreement of interpreters. Formal unity triumphed, but material unity was lost." Miranda (2003), p. 95.

[28] Identifying this issue, particularly with regard to the emphasis on efficiency (in a state model more focused on its outcomes), Offe points out that "efficiency here is not defined by adherence to rules, but rather by the fulfillment of functions and the attempt to produce effects. From the perspective of organizing its concrete tasks, the administration must variably arrange its own *inputs* and premises. It is efficient to the extent that it does so successfully. The premises of administrative action are no longer *rules* that must be followed without exception, but rather *resources*, evaluated in terms of their suitability for certain tasks." Subsequently, however, the same author argues that the enhancement of participatory mechanisms should serve to reinforce this state shift, stating that "social-state administrative policy becomes dependent on extra-legal legitimations, insofar as it ceases to be guided by legal *inputs*, making legal norms available in terms of their suitability; that is, this policy becomes dependent *either* on substantive and supra-legal ordering conceptions, *or* on empirical consensual processes (…) the task of achieving consensus and harmonizing interests arises for the administration (…) in its relationship with its own clientele." Offe (1984), pp. 221–225.

the Weimar Constitution of 1919.[29] In both, this more expansionist view of the State is formalized, bringing profound consequences for the legal field and its structure.

Indeed, this perspective has altered both the scope and the very nature of the interests to be protected by public authorities, conferring upon them legal significance. Whereas previously protection was afforded to interests characterized primarily by a negative aspect (requiring, in principle, less intervention by the state apparatus), this movement has led to the addition of more active and costly activities. This is the case with health and education, marking the transition between "generations" or "dimensions" of rights.[30]

Furthermore, throughout the twentieth century, these interests gradually came to assume a fundamental nature. While at first their provision might have seemed unusual and been regarded as a mere concession, developments in recent decades have placed the issue at the *core* of the legal framework. Following the terminology commonly used in our academic circles, this marked the transition from the Social State to the Constitutional State.

- The shift in the role of the State is accompanied by a change in constitutionally guaranteed rights, broadening their scope. In addition to the protection of property, elements such as the right to health and education are included.

In this context marked by numerous institutional changes, one might once again ask: Considering the reconfiguration of the public sphere and the legal domain,

[29] "With the First World War and the post-war period, States found themselves compelled to intervene in the economy (both in a regulatory capacity, through the enactment of mandatory rules governing private conduct, and in a managerial capacity, through the establishment of factories and industrial activities controlled by public entities). The first Constitution to address economic matters was the Mexican Constitution of 1917. However, it was the German Constitution of 1919, the 'Weimar Constitution,' that featured an entire chapter dedicated to the economic life of the nation. The phrase 'property entails obligations,' found in Article 153 of the Weimar Constitution, is a classic expression of this period. Thus, the State began to incorporate the economy into its primary directives and to intervene with increasing intensity in the economic domain. After all, as Comparato wrote, enshrining 'laissez faire' would amount to celebrating a 'laissez ne pas faire'—since the private economy no longer possessed sufficient strength. The leading economic theorist of this era was Keynes, whose works greatly influenced the forms of State intervention in the economy (…). It is from this point—the beginning of the twentieth century—that the economy becomes a matter of State, if not the most important one." Moreira (2006), pp. 104–105.

[30] The concept of "generations" of fundamental rights was introduced informally by Karel Vasak in 1979 during an inaugural lecture at the International Institute of Human Rights and gained prominence in legal scholarship for a considerable period—despite numerous criticisms, particularly regarding the lack of practical historicity that the concept appears to suggest. In other words, the main counterargument is that the notion of "generation" may lead to the belief that rights belonging to different categories do not accumulate; that is, with the emergence of second-generation rights, there would no longer be room for those of the first generation, and so on. This has led some, such as Ingo Sarlet, to replace the term with "dimension." In the author's words, "the dimensional theory of fundamental rights points not only to the cumulative nature of the evolutionary process and the complementary character of all fundamental rights, but also affirms, moreover, their unity and indivisibility within the context of domestic constitutional law." See Vasak (1979). Sarlet (2009), p. 46.

would it be possible for the official dispute resolution mechanism to remain unaffected? How has this series of value-based changes impacted civil procedure?

The answers become clear when we recall that the resolution of conflicts has become an essentially state function. Thus, changes in the social environment and in the nature of the State would naturally have effects on procedural law. With the adequacy of liberal values called into question, civil procedure would also have to seek new guiding principles and criteria.

In this way, just as the legal field was globally impacted by the expansion of state activity, dispute resolution was also influenced by this development. The discipline acquired a greater social function, recognizing that the interests at stake in disputes would be accompanied by a constant public interest[31]. There is a shift toward public law in the sense described by Antonio do Passo Cabral.[32]

Based on this premise, procedural issues arise that reflect this new value framework, shaping a State that is less neutral and more proactive. For example, it is now argued that the judge should be granted greater powers during the course of litigation, reflecting the State's own interest in the dispute. This results in a fundamental shift in areas such as civil enforcement or the production of evidence, substantially altering the subject matter.[33] And it could not be otherwise: with the establishment

[31] As described by Carlos Alberto Alvaro de Oliveira, "the liberal conception, not yet clearly imbued with the public character of proceedings, granted the parties not only broad powers to initiate and terminate the proceedings and to determine its subject matter, but also subjected its progress and development exclusively to their will, assigning them full responsibility with regard to the evidentiary phase itself. The powers of the judicial body were, therefore, significantly restricted (…) Today, however, the private character no longer corresponds to the prevailing conception of the nature and function of civil procedure, as experience has disproved the belief in the efficiency of the work carried out by the participants in the proceedings. It suffices to consider that the application of the dispositive principle in its classical conception, by imposing exclusive contribution of the parties in bringing factual matters to the proceedings, relativizes the judge's assessment of the truth beyond what is desirable, forcing the judge to passively accept the version presented by the parties. The adoption of the so-called system of legal proof also inconveniently restricts the freedom of the judicial body, given the strict regulation of the assessment of evidence, the most complete example of which is provided by common law." Oliveira (2003), p. 23.

[32] The term *publicismo* is recurrently used by the author to refer to a procedural structure whose institutions, in general terms, are characterized by the predominance of public values (rather than the exclusive interests of the parties). In this regard, the author notes that the essential features of this framework are: "(a) the State seeks to implement, through the proceedings, *public objectives* that *prevail* over the private interests of the parties and lead to the *mandatory application of statutory rules*, with the law considered the sole source of procedural norms; (b) the notion that *all procedural rules are of a public nature*, and therefore *mandatory, established in the public interest and not subject to derogation* by the will of the parties; the will of the litigants cannot decisively alter the course of the proceedings in a manner different from that provided by law; (c) rejection of the notion of proceedings as the "property of the parties" and the *expansion of the judge's* ex officio *powers*, especially in the conduct of the proceedings; the State-judge has become the central figure in the procedural legal relationship." Cabral (2016), p. 106.

[33] "The search for another working method, more consistent with the nature of the current procedure and capable of achieving greater efficiency in the application and realization of the law, is particularly embodied in the procedural reform carried out by FRANZ KLEIN in Austria at the close of the nineteenth century. After emphasizing the high value of the social and public function

of new demands, it is necessary to adapt the normative structure as well in order to avoid the risks of excessive formalism[34] or bureaucratic pathology.[35]

- The recognition that public authorities should act more proactively to protect rights, combined with the erosion of the neutrality dogma, brings new dimensions to the legal process. For example, issues such as the use of atypical techniques or procedural customization by judicial order become increasingly significant—granting greater powers to the judge.

2.3 Civil Procedure: Means and Ends

We have seen so far that civil procedure has been continuously evolving to reflect the changes occurring in its surrounding context. From liberalism and its specific values to the theoretical attempt to broaden participation in court proceedings, there is no procedural reform that is not influenced by its contextual background. In light

of procedure as revealed by history, KLEIN highlights the need to swiftly eradicate, in the simplest and most economical way, this genuine 'social evil' (*'sozial Übel'*). In this context, the procedural principles of orality, publicity, and the free evaluation of evidence are merely means—techniques, as we might say—to achieve the purpose of the procedure, understood as reliable and immediate assistance (*'Gegenwartshilfe'*), an indispensable institution for social welfare. From this premise, he derives above all the need for a more active role by the judge, who is called upon to participate more intensely in the proceedings and particularly in the investigation of facts. The aim is to entrust the judge with effective, not merely formal, direction of the procedure." OLIVEIRA, Carlos Alberto Alvaro de. Op. cit. p. 24. On this topic, see also the teaching of Álvaro Pérez Ragone, who argues that "The great influence demonstrated in the twentieth and twenty-first centuries in continental European systems is based on the Austrian Code of Civil Procedure of 1895, in which the principle of evidentiary contribution and party initiative is combined with the power of procedural direction vested in the judge. The premise is that the unlimited role of party autonomy may affect the establishment of facts, the determination of the truth, and, consequently, the allocation of cost and time truly necessary for a proceeding. The judge should not, in fact, assume a passive role in the face of strategic conduct and the exclusive and exclusionary direction of the parties. He is not a mere bystander, but the one who, at some point, must decide. Otherwise, according to Klein, it would be a case of a procedure without a Red Cross. On the contrary, the judge should assume a role, one that must be defined both in relation to the procedure and to those who participate in it." Ragone (2014), p. 243.

[34] According to Calamandrei, "the history of judicial institutions shows that the forms originally adopted to achieve certain ends tend to outlive their function (…) becoming ends in themselves; thus, at times, the purely instrumental value of the forms that should serve to facilitate justice degenerates into *formalism*, and they themselves become the object of blind worship." Calamandrei (1996), p. 322.

[35] "When an organization approaches the strategic model used as a normative framework, but in doing so puts its relationship with the environment at risk, we usually refer to bureaucratic pathologies, that is, the lack of correspondence between the internal structure and the external environment, or simply between structure and function." Cited from Offe (1984), p. 219.

of this, academia has developed various concepts aimed at explaining this movement, employing tools such as its segmentation into theoretical "phases."[36]

However, we believe that the issue can be more aptly summarized in another way. In our view, changes to the judicial process have essentially oscillated along a single axis: they either prioritize procedural means or material outcomes.[37] At its core, the debate ultimately mirrors the one identified by Carlos Ari Sundfeld in the field of Administrative Law: there are those who seek to "*tame the monster*" and those who aim to "*make it work.*"[38]

Understanding this aspect seems to us essential, as it decisively impacts the entire comprehension of civil procedure and is reflected in issues such as the scope afforded to its guarantees.[39] At its core, we believe there is always the same tug of war: on one side, the attempt to restrain state activity. On the other side, the pursuit of making it more effective. There is no debate related to procedure that does not encounter this logic, opposing the primacy of procedure to the primacy of the concrete effects of procedural action.[40]

With this background, the stage is set for us to present to the reader some other questions that may seem simple but are of utmost importance for understanding the subject: In order to pursue judicial effectiveness, should we have more procedure or less procedure? What are its pillars and foundations? What objectives does the analysis serve?

We believe that these provocations are relevant as they remind us that civil procedure can only be understood through the dialogue between its tools and its function—through the interplay between structure and action—reiterating a dilemma that is constant in society and demands ongoing efforts at reconciliation.[41]

---

[36] Dinamarco (1987).

[37] "While civil procedure is complex, and deals with many rules and exceptions, at its core are two fundamental ideas about the need for a system of justice to be both equitable and efficient. At the constitutional plane, those principles have been most fully developed in the *Mathews* line of cases. But to a large extent, even the technical aspects of the formal Rules of procedure are themselves simply expressions of these ideas (…)." Issacharoff (2005), p. 16.

[38] "There are professionals more focused on making the monster work: these see administrative law as the *law of public interest* (…) others fear the monster, want to tame it: they think of *law as control over power*." Sundfeld (2012).

[39] "Theories of procedural fairness and procedural rights fall into two broad categories: process-based and outcome-based. Process-based theories evaluate fairness by the way procedure treats litigants within the litigation process itself, independent of outcome quality. Outcome-based theories evaluate fairness by the quality of the outcomes a procedural system generates." Bone (2003), p. 189.

[40] "The problem has to do with the fact that adjudication is primarily about producing good outcomes, not about giving people a chance to participate and the opportunity in their lives to exercise autonomous choice (…) Why is outcome quality itself not sufficient for legitimacy?" Bone (2003), p. 193.

[41] "The problem of the relation between the individual and society, or between action and social structure, lies at the heart of social theory and the philosophy of social science. In the writings of most major theorists, from Marx, Weber, and Durkheim to a variety of contemporary authors, this problem is raised and allegedly resolved in one way or another. Such resolutions generally amount

- Thus, it only makes sense to investigate whether more procedures are desired if one has in mind what it is intended for, allowing for a serious discussion about its improvement. The issue is objective. While it is impossible to develop a given tool without questioning its scope, that scope can only be achieved if the available instrument is adequate. These spheres are complementary, which is why one cannot be understood without the other.

This line of reasoning is frequently employed in the public sector as a gauge of legitimacy, engaging with the very issues discussed in the previous sections. Thus, it is understandable that in an essentially liberal environment, public instruments were guided by the prevailing standards of the time (security, predictability, and neutrality), just as the expansion of the welfare state required adaptations and new approaches. Overall, this trajectory reveals the ongoing attempt to harmonize *objectives* and *means, purposes* and *techniques,* and, ultimately, *function* and *structure.*

Within the scope of civil procedure, this same logic also leads to an incessant attempt at dialogue: the demand for greater predictability and security has shaped institutions guided by these values; the search for a more protective state has led to procedural alternatives compatible with this perspective; the call for a more dialogical approach has fostered the enhancement of participation in court proceedings. In short, a continuous and unending movement is formed in pursuit of legitimacy.

Thus, to address the issues raised above, it is essential to take a step back: after all, what is expected of civil procedural law? Only after defining this functional framework can any aspect related to the mechanisms of operation in this field be examined and developed. Only then is it possible to determine whether we need more or less procedure or more or less formality.

With this broader perspective, we also observe that the very concept of "*effectiveness*" is quite flexible, subject to ongoing interpretive development. As a result, it is necessary to recognize the argumentative nature of this quality criterion. Only by considering the functional role assigned to the discipline will it be possible to define its contours in a reflective and ongoing process.

In this regard, advocating for an expansion of the proceedings may be appropriate for those who place greater emphasis on procedural means, thereby enhancing aspects related to participation. Conversely, the attempt to streamline the judicial process would tend to be a suitable alternative for those who prioritize values such as speed and efficiency. The decisive step, it seems to us, always begins with the same question: What is the purpose of the proceedings? This should be the leitmotif guiding any reform or adaptation of the legal framework. Coherence is necessary, harmonizing premises and conclusions.

- To conclude the chapter with an illustrative example: if the proceedings are viewed primarily as an environment focused on participation, it is likely that

---

to the accentuation of one term at the expense of the other (...) few questions in social theory remain as refractory to cogent analysis as the question of how, and in precisely what ways, the action of individual agents is related to the structural features of the societies of which they are part." Thompson (2003), p. 56.

efforts will be made to expand the evidentiary phase, maximize the adversarial process, and grant the parties broad freedom in presenting evidence. If, on the other hand, the outcome is considered paramount, this type of procedural element would end up being more strictly conditioned by a necessarily functional approach.

References

Berger, P. L., & Berger, B. (1977). O que é uma instituição social? In M. M. Foracchi & J. S. Martins (Eds.), *Sociologia e Sociedade: Leitura de introdução à Sociologia*. LTC.

Bobbio, N. (1995). *O Positivismo Jurídico*. Ícone.

Bobbio, N. (2000). *Igualdade e Liberdade* (4th ed.). Ediouro.

Bone, R. G. (2003). *The economics of civil procedure*. Foundation Press.

Cabral, A. P. (2016). *Convenções Processuais*. Juspodivm.

Calamandrei, P. (1996). *Instituciones de derecho procesal civil* (Vol. 1). El Foro.

Clève, C. M. (1995). A Teoria Constitucional e o Direito Alternativo (por uma dogmática constitucional emancipatória). In C. Lembo (Ed.), *Uma vida dedicada ao Direito – Homenagem a Carlos Henrique de Carvalho*. Ed. RT.

Comparato, F. K. (1965). O indispensável direito econômico. *Revista dos Tribunais, 353*.

Costa, P. (2006). O Estado de Direito: uma introdução histórica. In P. Costa & D. Zolo (Eds.), *O Estado de Direito: história, teoria e crítica*. Martins Fontes.

Couture, E. J. (1942). *Fundamentos del Derecho Procesal Civil*. Aniceto Lopez Editor.

Dinamarco, C. R. (1987). *A instrumentalidade do processo*. Ed. RT.

Durkheim, E. (2007). *As regras do método sociológico*. Martins Fontes.

Gomes, O. (2010). *Direitos Reais* (20th ed.). Forense.

Grossi, P. (2005). *Primeiras lições sobre o Direito*. Forense.

Hespanha, A. M. (2005). *Cultura Jurídica Europeia*. Boiteux.

Hespanha, A. M. (2012). *O Caleidoscópio do Direito*. Almedina.

Issacharoff, S. (2005). *Civil procedure*. Foundation Press.

Keynes, J. M. (1936). *The general theory of employment, interest and money*. Palgrave Macmillan.

Kuttner, R. (1992). *The end of laissez-faire—National purpose and the global economy after the cold war*. University of Pennsylvania Press.

Marinoni, L. G. (2005). *Teoria Geral do Processo*. Ed. RT.

Marinoni, L. G., Arenhart, S. C., & Mitidiero, D. (2015a). *Novo Curso de Processo Civil—Tutela dos Direitos Mediante Procedimentos Diferenciados*. Ed. RT.

Marinoni, L. G., Arenhart, S. C., & Mitidiero, D. (2015b). *Novo Curso de Processo Civil—Teoria do Processo Civil*. Ed. RT.

Marinoni, L. G., Ragone, A. P., & Ojeda, R. N. (2010). *Fundamentos del proceso civil - Hacia una teoría de la adjudicación*. Abeledo Perrot.

Miranda, J. (2003). *Manual de Direito Constitucional* (Vol. 1, 7th ed.). Coimbra Editora.

Mitidiero, D. (2011). *Colaboração no processo civil: pressupostos sociais, lógicos e éticos* (2nd ed.). Ed. RT.

Moreira, E. B. (2006). Os princípios constitucionais da atividade econômica. *Revista da Faculdade de Direito da UFPR,.45*.

Offe, C. (1984). Critérios de racionalidade e problemas funcionais da ação político-administrativa. In C. Offe (Ed.), *Problemas Estruturais do Estado Capitalista*. Tempo Brasileiro.

Oliveira, C. A. A. (2003). Poderes do Juiz e Visão Cooperativa do Processo. Genesis. *Revista de Direito Processual Civil, 27*.

Pasquino, P. (2001). One and three: Separation of powers and the Independence of the judiciary in the Italian constitution. In J. Ferejohn, J. N. Kakove, & J. Riley (Eds.), *Constitutional culture and democratic rule*. Cambridge University Press.
Ragone, A. P. (2014). Retrato del revisionismo garantista en el proceso civil a través de Klein y Wach. *Revista de Processo, 233*.
Ripert, G. (1947). *Aspectos jurídicos do capitalismo moderno*. Freitas Bastos.
Sarlet, I. W. (2009). *A eficácia dos direitos fundamentais—uma teoria geral dos direitos fundamentais na perspectiva constitucional* (10th ed.). Livraria do Advogado.
Sarlet, I. W., Marinoni, L. G., & Mitidiero, D. (2012). *Curso de Direito Constitucional*. Ed. RT.
Scott, J. L. (1998). *Seeing like a state: How certain schemes to improve the human condition have failed*. Yale University Press.
Silva, O. A. B. (2000). *Curso de Processo Civil* (Vol. 1, 5th ed.). Ed. RT.
Silva, O. A. B., & Gomes, F. (2010). *Teoria Geral do Processo* (5th ed.). Ed. RT.
Sundfeld, C. A. (2012). *Direito Administrativo para Céticos*. Ed. RT.
Talamini, E. (2015). Arbitragem e a Tutela Provisória no Código de Processo Civil de 2015. *Revista de Arbitragem e Mediação, 46*.
Thompson, J. B. (2003). The theory of structuration. In J. B. Thompson & D. Held (Eds.), *Social theory of modern society: Anthony Giddens and his critics*. Cambridge University Press.
Vasak, K. (1979). For the third generation of human rights: The rights of solidarity. *International Institute of Human Rights*, July.
Weber, M. (2002). A política como vocação. In H. H. Gerth & C. W. Mills (Eds.), *Ensaios de sociologia*. LTC.

Chapter 3
Why Critically Analyze Civil Procedure?

3.1 Civil Procedure as a Cultural Issue

The discussions presented in the previous chapter reveal to the reader that civil procedure cannot be depicted as a static framework, but rather as a work in constant motion. In summary, this field is characterized by its flexibility, adapting to the needs present in its environment. Consequently, an essential foundation for its critical analysis emerges: the fact that the mechanism adopted for dispute resolution in each society represents a cultural phenomenon.

In a didactic manner, the discussion of this aspect can begin with a few thought-provoking questions. Why do different countries exhibit such distinct approaches to conflict resolution? What leads to such varying degrees of importance being attributed to elements like the Jury Trial or the evidentiary hearing, even in seemingly proximate regions? Is this kind of divergence normal? How should this issue influence the study of procedural law?

The questions above corroborate the flexible nature of procedural law. Furthermore, each of them leads to the same conclusion: civil procedure is also a cultural expression. In summary, the method of dispute resolution established in a given place will reflect its own culture, adding a new piece to the puzzle.[1]

[1] Summarizing this idea, Daniel Mitidiero states that "it is commonplace in the study of law, and increasingly so within the field of civil procedure, to assert that law is intimately intertwined with the experience and culture of the people (…) that is to say: experience, as a fact gathered from the continuous and inscrutable practice of life, and culture, 'considered as the set of spiritual and material experiences that distinguish a particular era of a society,' in the classic definition by Galeno Lacerda, inform and shape the law (…) this relationship between law and culture becomes even more evident if we seek to highlight it in the context of civil procedural law." See Mitidiero (2004), p. 485. In the same vein, and supporting the author, see the framework presented in Lacerda (1961).

G. Osna, *Civil Procedure, Culture, and Proportionality*,
https://doi.org/10.1007/978-3-032-27555-4_3

This observation, inherent to the thinking of Chase and Taruffo, challenges the theorist to take a step back.[2] After all, only by establishing what is meant by *culture* is it possible to assess its relevance to the legal process. The issue is logical in nature: it is impossible to claim that a particular piece of music has *mojo* without first knowing what *mojo* is. Moreover, this touches on one of the most controversial aspects of anthropology and contemporary society, which cannot be fully addressed here.[3]

Thus, in an instrumental sense, we understand *culture* as a broad and contextual arrangement, composed of the ideas, values, and institutions generally accepted within a given environment.[4] It is within this amalgam of vectors that its *cultural milieu* resides. The urgency of this web has profound effects on the legal process: if the procedural system *reflects* the culture in which it is situated, it must constantly adapt to its changes.

- As an example, it is on this premise that Chase justifies the prominent role given to the jury institution in the United States. There, the issue is *cultural*, dating back to the period of English colonization and the settlers' struggle for the possibility of self-government. In this sense, trial by peers would serve as a measure to contain state power and disperse authority, finding support in American culture and its historical development.[5]

---

[2] On this point, see Chase (2014). See also Taruffo (2009).

[3] On this subject, see Geertz (1973), with particular emphasis on the framework developed therein. Similarly, summarizing the issue and demonstrating the underlying divergence (Edwards, 2007). Also, Muller (2005). Minkov (2012).

[4] In the words of Chase, "I adopt a concept of culture that links common points which persist over time, though they are hardly eternal, and which are widely, though not uniformly, shared by a determinable collectivity. To quote Kroeber and Kluckhohn, 'the essential core of culture consists of traditional ideas (i.e., those historically derived and selected) and especially their attached values; cultural systems may, on the one hand, be considered as products of action, and on the other, as conditioning elements of future action.' More specifically, the definition of culture used here includes 'traditional ideas, values, and norms' that are widely shared within a social group. Culture encompasses propositions about beliefs that are both normative ('killing is wrong except when authorized by the State') and cognitive ('the Earth is round'). Culture also includes the symbols that represent the spirit of its people (the figure of Justice with her scales; a globe on a desk)." Chase (2014), p. 26.

[5] "It is striking and revealing that the American egalitarian ethos and the jury, as a mechanism for the protection of individual rights, developed together. The veneration of the jury in American life emerged at the same time as the people embraced their exceptionalist values. It was around the time of the American Revolution that the jury became 'so deeply rooted in the American democratic ethos.' By the mid-eighteenth century, as Americans were progressively distinguishing themselves as a unique people, juries became a means of resisting the Crown's control over colonial affairs, which is why the British attempt to limit the powers of the institution was a motivating factor for grievances. Since then, stories of jurors who bravely opposed the tyrannical English government have become part of the American self-image: 'most American history books point to the [John Peter] Zenger libel trial in 1735 as the paradigmatic case for freedom of the press and as an example of the people's victory over the aristocracy' (…) Although the hagiography surrounding the Zenger case has produced a questionable idealization of its participants, the litigation

- This concern would also be at the core of the evidentiary procedure model adopted in U.S. civil proceedings. Here, too, the content is guided by the reduction of the role of the courts and their management capacity. Ultimately, the structure of *discovery* is linked to the very attempt to mitigate state power and its interventionism, granting greater autonomy to private parties.[6] Drawing on Damaška's ideas, its codification would represent a step in a *coordinated* direction, reinforcing this feature within the social sphere.[7]
- The same line of reasoning also explains why societies more inclined toward *dialogue* and *solidarity* place greater emphasis on dispute resolution models oriented toward *mediation* and *conciliation*.[8] In such cases, the importance of the litigants to the social context suggests that the conflict should not produce losers; both parties continue to play an essential role, justifying the avoidance of rifts that could undermine this mechanism.[9]

'helped to establish particularly American views about the jury and its place between the law and the people.'" Chase (2014), pp. 88–89.

[6] "Individualism, egalitarianism, laissez-faire, and anti-statism are also evident in another practice related to dispute resolution that is particularly strong in the United States and is not replicated with the same impact anywhere else: *pretrial discovery*. This is a power granted to the parties to control the investigation of facts before trial. Again, the contrast is even more pronounced when the United States is compared with continental systems." Chase (2014), p. 91.

[7] In the words of the author, "while to coordinate authority it is perfectly acceptable to allow private attorneys to take oral depositions in their private offices, the hierarchical process does not even have a categorical niche to classify this practice. At first, when viewed through the spectacles of hierarchical authority, the taking of oral depositions appears as a mere private interview aimed at developing the lawsuit (…) yet because more than a private interview is involved, depositions tend to be viewed as an arrogation by private persons of action that must be reserved for governmental officials. Quite predictably, attempts by American attorneys to conduct depositions on the Continent are treated there as offensive to the prerogative of the state to administer justice and are now outlawed in several European countries." Damaška (1986), p. 67.

[8] After all, as Auerbach points out, "understanding communities through their methods of dispute resolution may seem idiosyncratic. But this perspective gives us access to a complex and recurring cultural dialogue: between individuals and the community; between the aspiration for harmony and the reality of conflict; between formal legal institutions and their alternatives. Every society experiences this tension. It is important to understand that preferences for modes of conflict resolution are not final choices, but rather evolving commitments. Even in the most deeply legalistic society, there is likely to be a constant movement over time: between the constraints of the formal legal system and the appeal of informal alternatives. In fact, once the old customary order (based on a group's shared moral vision) is in decline, the main shift is toward explicit legal rules and procedures 'that clarify what the disintegration of the community has rendered obscure and uncertain.'" Auerbach (2007), p. 46.

[9] "Community alternatives to judicial litigation invite reflection on disputes as a form of social behavior. The nature of dispute processes ultimately arises from a delicate interaction between personal relationships within a given social structure. The choice made by disputants—whether to ignore their differences, negotiate, submit the conflict to mediation or arbitration, or retain lawyers with a view to litigation—is highly significant. The way people engage in disputes depends, after all, on how (and if) they relate to one another. In intimate, affectionate, and reciprocal relationships, disputants will behave quite differently toward their opponents than they would if those opponents were strangers or adversaries. Selfishness and aggressiveness do not depend merely on

The mindset inherent in each case demonstrates that culture and procedure are in constant synchrony. Thus, it becomes evident that the uncritical importation of any tool from comparative law should be approached with caution[10]: Civil procedure

individual personality: they are socially sanctioned—or discouraged. Similarly, there is also a social component in the choice between defining the other party as an adversary and fighting until there is a clear winner and loser, or, alternatively, resolving the conflict in a way that preserves, rather than destroys, the relationship." Auerbach (2007), p. 47. Furthermore, some authors argue that the same phenomenon may operate in the opposite direction, maintaining that the valorization of self-composition methods could also transform the parties and reduce their litigiousness. This is, in fact, the central premise of so-called "transformative" mediation, originally articulated by Folger and Bush, which holds that this approach to dispute resolution can have deeper effects than merely achieving an efficient settlement of the case. In summary, it is argued that the geometric recomposition of the dispute and the empowerment granted to the parties during the judicial process would provide new perspectives for debate and reflection, impacting the very lives of the individuals involved and their perception of the conflict. In the words of the theorists, "the transformative theory starts from the premise that interactional crisis is what conflict means to people. And help in overcoming that crisis is a major part of what parties want from a mediator. According to this view, what would transformative theory expect people like Jim and Susan to say about the family business conflict mentioned earlier in this chapter, if they were asked questions such as these: 'What affects you most about this conflict you're involved in? What's the impact that seems to strike you hardest?'" And from this, the following conclusion is reached: "What kind of help do people want from a mediator? As transformative theory sees it, with solid support from research on conflict, parties who come to mediators are looking for—and valuing—more than an efficient way to reach agreements on specific issues. They are looking for a way to change and transform their destructive conflict interaction into a more positive one, to the greatest degree possible, so that they can move on with their lives constructively, whether together or apart." See Bush and Folger (2005), pp. 45–53.

[10] Note that, in highlighting the possible gulf between modern law and ethnolaw, the author acknowledges that "outside our cultural framework, it may occur that the judge takes into account, in a more flexible manner, the position of the parties before and during the proceedings. The degree of sympathy and the consensus of the community (which is achieved by adapting to the socially accepted scale of values) is also relevant with respect to judicial outcomes. In other contexts, the judgment will aim to reinforce social cohesion, which is achieved by favoring, in the proceedings, the stronger party, who will not lack the power and means necessary to enforce the decision, without this giving rise to destabilizing disagreements. In others, there is concern for the individual, whose judgment should take place on a supernatural level (ordeal judgment), or, alternatively, extra-sensory truths will be investigated, resorting to magical-type procedures. Notwithstanding the (indeed, because of the) diversity between the reality of non-literate peoples and the reality we find in developed countries, anthropological experience constitutes for the comparatist a unique practice, because it teaches numerous fundamental truths and, above all, protects him from dangerous errors and prejudices." Sacco (2001), pp. 48–49.

cannot be detached from its context, as it is subject to this *habitus*[11]. It arises from a specific cultural environment and is also an integral part of it.[12]

In light of this, we gain a clearer understanding of why neighboring countries address the same procedural issues in different ways. This is evident, for example, in the assessment of evidence in Brazil and Chile,[13] or in the regulation of injunctive relief in the Brazilian and Peruvian legal systems.[14] It is also apparent in the hearing

---

[11] As stated by Bourdieu, "objectified, institutionalized history only becomes *enacted* and effective if the position (…) finds, as if it were a suit or a house, someone who finds it interesting and sees advantages in it, someone who recognizes themselves in it enough to take responsibility for it and assume it. This means that so many actions, not only those of the official identified with their function, present themselves as ceremonies through which agents – who are not, for that reason, *actors* playing *roles* – step into the social character expected of them and which they expect of themselves (…) and this by virtue of the immediate and total *coincidence* of *habitus* and habit that makes the true monk. The café waiter does not play at being a café waiter (…) his body, in which a history is inscribed, *marries* his function, that is, a history, a tradition, which he has only ever seen embodied in bodies or, better yet, in those garments *inhabited* by a certain *habitus* we call café waiters." Bourdieu (1989), pp. 87–88.

[12] "Judicial proceedings become ritualized through repetition: a way of acting becomes the correct way to act. 'Ritual action is repetitive and therefore generally redundant, but this element plays an essential role in channeling emotions, providing cognitive orientation, and organizing social groups.' This occurs through participation. 'By following rituals, behaviors become beliefs.' Or, as Geertz puts it, we move 'from how we ought to act given our beliefs to what our beliefs ought to be given how we act.' Belief precedes and conditions action, and action also conditions belief. The dispute resolution process is designed to reaffirm the beliefs that underlie it and that, through action, are externalized within it." Chase (2014), p. 179.

[13] "With regard to the means of evidence, the Chilean Code of Civil Procedure, in its Article 341 (330), establishes that these are: (a) documents (Instrumentos); (b) witnesses (Testigos); (c) confession (Confesión de parte); (d) judicial inspection (Inspección personal del Tribunal); (e) expert evidence (Informes de peritos); and (f) presumptions (Presunciones). As for testimonial evidence, what drew our attention in the Chilean procedure is precisely what is set forth in Article 363. See the article, literally transcribed: 'Art. 363 (352) Before examining each witness, he or she shall be required to take an oath in the following terms: "Do you swear by God to tell the truth about what you are about to be asked?" The person questioned shall answer: "Yes, I swear," in accordance with the provisions of the article.' Although we have the notion that there has already been a separation between State and Religion, there are still remnants of a past in which State and Religion walked hand in hand, and religious morality dictated rules of lawful conduct. Swearing by God at the moment of testimony is a clear example of the State's connection to Religion (…) We will not dwell here on the elements of evidence indicated in the Chilean Code of Civil Procedure, but we must highlight an issue that we do not clearly observe in the Brazilian Code of Civil Procedure, namely, the express indication of presumption as a means of evidence (…) Finally, regarding evidence, it should be noted that the principle governing the Chilean Code of Civil Procedure is that of material truth, and this principle is made explicit insofar as there is a literal provision that, when there are two contradictory pieces of evidence, the judge must resolve the issue always seeking the truth (…) In the name of material truth, Article 429 states that, to invalidate a public deed with witnesses, five witnesses are required. This demonstrates the evidentiary tariff system admitted in Chilean civil procedure." Soares (2012), pp. 325–326.

[14] Identifying the Peruvian reality, Christian Delgado Suarez states that "in Peruvian procedural law, at the doctrinal, jurisprudential, and legislative levels, there is no concern for establishing a special procedure aimed at preventing an unlawful act or removing its harmful effects that persist over time. In the absence of such a procedure, the structure of Peruvian civil procedure is domi-

systems currently in force in Germany and Italy,[15] or in the models of class actions adopted by different European countries.[16] In all these cases, the structural differences are far greater than geographical proximity might suggest.

However, despite the importance of these examples, the explanation becomes clearer when we once again turn to the thinking of Oscar Chase. This is because the author *radicalizes* the issue, setting aside the comparison between similar models

---

nated by the full and exhaustive cognition process, so that an inhibitory action may be filed, which will conclude with a condemnatory judgment. Only after the judgment becomes final and proceeds to execution can it be enforced using executive techniques that are, at present, nonexistent in the Peruvian Code of Civil Procedure of 1993. In order to illustrate the lack of care and interest in the protection of rights, the Constitutional Court of Peru unfortunately ruled that 'when, as a consequence of the exercise of informational freedoms, other fundamental rights such as those relating to honor and image are violated, the protection of the latter cannot amount to a preventive measure against a media outlet to prevent it from disseminating information that may be considered harmful.' In truth, if the very guardian of the Peruvian Constitution fails to recognize the inviolability of the very rights it is meant to protect, it thereby enacts a self-denial of its own essence in this regard." Suarez (2013), p. 317

[15] Explaining the issue, Rolf Stürner and Christoph Kern state that, on one hand, there is a prevailing "Italo-Canonical" model, a "traditional civil law model, as exists in continental Europe and in many countries influenced by these legal systems during the first two-thirds of the twentieth century. Today, its representatives are France, Italy, and the vast majority of Latin American countries. The introductory phase of this model (…) consists of a claim and a response. However, in this model, there is some uncertainty regarding the form of the claim: is it merely a notice, or should the facts be described? Sometimes a simple notice suffices, but at times a detailed description of the facts and the claim is required (…) the content of the intermediate or interim phase (…) consists of a sequence of hearings held before an investigating judge and the presentation of evidence on disputed points. Everything that occurs serves as information for the judiciary, which soon becomes fully involved in the proceedings." On the other hand, there is the "main hearing model," "a recent innovation that has emerged among these models based on their structure. Interestingly, it has attracted followers from all legal families: Germany and modern Spain, representing the civil law countries of the Romano-Germanic family, and, at least to some extent today, England, which is the quintessential common law country. The introductory phase requires more than a mere notice, involving fact pleading, so that the defendant and the judiciary know from the outset the contours of the case. The second phase of the proceedings, the interim or preparatory phase, is when the parties and the judge seek to determine the applicable law, the precise factual basis of the dispute, and the available means of evidence (…) the main hearing, which constitutes the third phase of the proceedings, begins with the presentation of the results from the previous phase. Evidence is then produced, and issues not clarified during the preparatory phase are addressed." Stürner and Kern (2011), pp. 211–213.

[16] In fact, after carefully analyzing the different national models in existence, Christopher Hodges concludes that, despite the strength of community regulation, there is no consensus among European countries on the subject. In the author's words, "a number of European states have introduced collective mechanisms for claims for damages. The number of states who have so far taken this step is limited, albeit growing, and the model adopted has been different in each case. There is no absolute uniformity or harmonization of approach, although some similarities exist (…) an immediate conclusion is that any EU enthusiast bent on furthering harmonization of national civil procedure rules or introducing a harmonized approach to collective damages claims would currently face what appears to be an insurmountable challenge in proposing a maximum harmonization model. A 'one size fits all' approach is simply not possible in relation to collective mechanisms." Hodges (2008), p. 86.

and using the *Azande* tribe as a reference point. It is through the observation of this community that the North American parallel would reach its limit. Much like water and oil, the differences would appear to be irreconcilable, precluding any form of convergence.

In summary, the author meticulously demonstrates how the *Azande* provided a prominent role for magic within their society. In various social spheres, this small tribe located in Central Africa adopted witchcraft as a guiding principle for action, granting it a position of significance. The resolution of disputes was no exception, also possessing a predominantly *oracular* nature.

This issue is elucidated by Evans-Pritchard, who explains that among the various forms of *witchcraft* that served as a kind of *legal process* in that civilization, the most valuable was provided by the *benge* poison oracle.[17] To us, its essence might seem quite simple and rudimentary: in the face of conflict, a small dose of poison (*benge*) was administered to a chick, and its reaction was observed.[18] For them, however, the outcome carried a sign from the divine: the death or survival of the animal represented an act of the oracle, expressing its will regarding the dispute.[19] This would be the decisive factor in determining the result.

[17] In the words of Evans-Pritchard, "the poison oracle, *benge,* is by far the most important of the Zande oracles. The Zande rely completely on its decisions, which have the force of law when obtained on the orders of a prince. A visitor to Zandeland hears as much about the poison oracle as he does about witchcraft, for whenever a question arises regarding the facts of a case or a man's well-being, they immediately seek to know the opinion of the poison oracle on the matter. In many situations where we seek to base a verdict upon evidence or try to regulate our conduct by weighing probabilities, the Zande consult, without hesitation, the poison oracle and follow its directions with implicit trust. No important venture is undertaken without the authorization of the poison oracle. In major collective undertakings, in all life crises, in all serious legal disputes, in all matters strongly affecting individual welfare—in short, on all occasions regarded by the Azande as dangerous or socially significant—the activity is preceded by consultation of the poison oracle." Evans-Pritchard (1976), pp. 121–122.

[18] "The method of revealing what is hidden by administering poison to fowls is widespread in Africa; but just as the Azande are the most north-easterly people who conceive of witchcraft as a material substance in the belly, so too is their culture the north-eastern limit of the distribution of this type of oracle. They are the only people in the Anglo-Egyptian Sudan who use it. The poison employed is a red powder made from a forest creeper and mixed with water to form a paste. The liquid is squeezed from the paste into the beaks of small domestic fowls, which are forced to swallow it. Generally, violent spasms follow. The doses are sometimes fatal, but just as often the fowls recover. Sometimes they are even unaffected by the poison. From the behavior of the fowls during this ordeal, especially their death or survival, the Azande receive answers to the questions they put to the oracle. The botanical nature of the poison has not been determined, but its chemical nature has been roughly analyzed." Evans-Pritchard (1976), pp. 121–122.

[19] In Chase's account, "after questioning the accused as to whether they would accept the judgment of the oracle, to which they promptly assented, the chief would order that the matter be referred to the benge and that the session be adjourned. The consultation with the benge would take place outside the court a few days later. An attendant would hold a chick and force it to swallow a small amount of a fluid containing the mystical benge, a ritually prepared toxic substance. An interrogator would then address the oracle in simple terms: 'Oracle, if (so-and-so) slept with (so-and-so), and if he knew her as a man, (etc.), let the chick die.' The question was repeated several times in a ritualistic form of speech. The chick died, thus proving to the satisfaction of the interrogator that

With this general outline in mind, an initial reaction of surprise would dismiss any possibility that the contemporary continental process might bear similarities to the *Azande* model. On one hand, there is a structure ostensibly guided by the possibility of participation and technical rationality. On the other hand, there is something that, to us, is limited to a random ordeal. These are two seemingly opposite scenarios, with no common ground or points of convergence.

However, adopting a critical perspective on the issue, we understand that this appearance is deceptive and that the gap between the models is not as deep as one might suppose. This is because, whether in our legal process or in the Zande spell, the central problem to be addressed is precisely the same: the search for contextual legitimacy.[20] In other words, both systems seek the acceptance of the community. They strike the same note, but are tuned to the audience's taste.

Thus, considering that for its recipients a decision based on *benge* would have possessed a divine character, the fact that it may seem irrational to us today is of little consequence. After all, such incredulity would certainly be mutual: if a Zande from that period were brought to present-day Latin America, the existence of a procedural model that disregards the oracular will would undoubtedly strike him as equally strange. Hart's criterion for composing his rule of recognition applies precisely here,[21] and it is worth noting that the distinction between the internal and external observer is also relevant to the legal process.[22] Here as well, it is internal

adultery had occurred. The oracle was consulted again, this time regarding the conduct of the defendant, with the same result." Chase (2014), p. 38.

[20] According to Gilley, "the concept of political legitimacy is central to virtually all of political science because it pertains to how power may be used in ways that citizens consciously accept (…) political legitimacy is a major determinant of both the structure and operation of states. There is a general presumption that its absence has profound implications for the way that states behave toward citizens and others. States that lack legitimacy devote more resources to maintaining their rule and less to effective governance, which reduces support and makes them vulnerable to overthrow or collapse. Within the ruling elite, doubts about legitimacy undermine self-esteem, which creates splits that accelerate this process. More generally, the concept has become a central part of modern political discourse, perhaps owing to the emancipatory impact of globalization. In our global era, states that rely only on coercion or individual payoffs are unstable. From apartheid South Africa to crony-ridden Indonesia, illegitimate regimes have been quickly replaced by unaccepting societies. Nothing will turn heads more than a cry of 'legitimacy crisis.'" Gilley (2006), p. 499.

[21] According to Hart, "the simple form of remedy for the uncertainty of some of the regime's primary rules is the introduction of what we shall call a 'rule of recognition' (…) the existence of such a rule of recognition may take any of a huge variety of forms, simple or complex (…) this is not the crucial step, though it is a very important one: what is crucial is the acknowledgment of reference to the writing or inscription as authoritative, i.e., as the proper way of disposing of doubts as to the existence of the rule." Expounding on this issue, Bruno Torrano notes that "in this context, Hart's rule of recognition emerges as the secondary norm that, by resolving the problem of legal *uncertainty*, ultimately determines which legal rules are binding in a given community. It is, therefore, the norm that confers the seal of legality upon other norms." See Hart (1988), p. 92; Torrano (2014), p. 129.

[22] "The use of unstated rules of recognition, by courts and others, in identifying particular rules of the system is characteristic of the internal point of view. Those who use them in this way thereby

acceptance that will lead the dispute resolution system to be legitimately accepted and thus capable of enduring.[23]

Understood in this way, we observe that the similarity between the *Azande* judgment and our civil procedure is greater than one might think. Both serve their respective cultural environments, internalizing and reproducing them. Two poles whose difference once seemed radical are thus brought closer together in reasoning that could equally be applied to any other locality. Regardless of the place, procedural law carries with it a constant need for *legitimation.*

- Against this backdrop, the current role of the proceduralist can be likened to that of a conductor who takes charge of the orchestra in the midst of a performance—leading various musicians and capable of presenting anything from operas to tribal rhythms. In this context, the decisive filter will be acceptance itself, and the risk will always be the same: that the conductor disregards the audience, playing only the music he personally wishes to hear. In such a case, the gap between theory and reality is likely to exact its toll.

3.2 The Judicial Process: Concepts and Rituals

The above reflections demonstrate that, at first glance, the notion of "civil procedure" allows for different interpretations and critical analyses. As discussed, its construction involves a space for creative freedom and the pursuit of legitimate acceptance. However, when we turn our attention to the Western context, this

manifest their own acceptance of them as guiding rules, and with this attitude there comes a characteristic vocabulary different from the natural expressions of the external point of view. Perhaps the simplest of these is the expression, 'It is the law that ...,' which we may find not only on the lips of judges, but also of ordinary people living under a legal system, when they identify a given rule of the system (...) this attitude of shared acceptance of rules is to be contrasted with that of an observer who records ab extra the fact that a social group accepts such rules but does not himself accept them. The natural expression of this external point of view is not 'It is the law that...,' but 'In England they recognize as law...whatever the Queen in Parliament enacts.' The first of these forms of expression we shall call an internal statement because it manifests the internal point of view and is naturally used by one who, accepting the rule of recognition and without stating the fact that it is accepted, applies the rule in recognizing some particular rule of the system as valid. The second form of expression we shall call an external statement because it is the natural language of an external observer of the system who, without himself accepting its rule of recognition, states the fact that others accept it." Hart (1988), p. 99.

[23] Here, it is worth noting Tamanaha's caveat regarding the very legitimacy of the primacy of the *rule of law*. In his words, "in order for the rule of law to exist, people must believe in and be proper and existing part of their political-legal system. This attitude is not itself a legal rule. It is a shared political ideal that amounts to a cultural belief. When this cultural belief is pervasive, the rule of law can be resilient, spanning generations and surviving episodes in which the rule of law is flouted by government officials. When this cultural belief is not pervasive, however, the rule of law ends up being either weak or non-existent." Tamanaha (2009), pp. 10–11.

criterion still appears to lead to two potentially problematic extremes: rituals and concepts.

After all, why do we wear robes in our courts? Is this attire a custom of our society? And what about the vocabulary used in court sessions? Are linguistic expressions such as "Your Excellency" or "Honorable" part of our everyday language? Does the use of Latin, common in the legal sphere, have the same support in social settings?

The questions highlight the strength of ritual in our dispute resolution, exposing a legacy that may now be anachronistic. Furthermore, its presence reveals a kind of convergence between the sacred and procedural.[24] From the imposing buildings that house our Courts to the peculiarities of their operation, an image of inviolability and wisdom is created[25]—reinforcing a separation between professionals and laypeople.

- The legitimacy of the proceedings, therefore, often arises from undeclared and symbolic elements. When citizens observe its imposing buildings and complex language, they feel vulnerable before the judiciary—and thus, unable to challenge it.

In the same way, it is also common for continental civil procedural law to seek legitimacy in broad concepts. In this regard, notions such as "guarantee of action," "due process," "adversarial proceedings," or "access to justice" serve as true triggers, aiming to imbue the dispute resolution mechanism with adequacy and soundness. As a result, there is a risk of overlooking the interpretive nature of each of these principles, turning them into immutable dogmas.

---

[24] "Whether in the Supreme Court of the United States or in a state court, a judge will almost never perform judicial duties without a black robe, a garment whose other uses in American reality are generally limited to similarly ceremonial events, such as those of a religious or academic nature. The robe thus implicitly signals that its wearer possesses both knowledge and a divine task, and that the occasion carries a sense of special significance. Another relevant aspect is the setting. The trial takes place in a specifically designated location that deliberately incorporates culturally recognizable expressions of power. The judge's chair is higher and more imposing than any other in the room, so that anyone addressing the judge must "look up." The courtroom itself is rarely anything less than a grand structure (…) For an attentive juror, this inscription, set in brushed metal amid the wooden structure behind the judge, "confirms the sacred architecture: the altar as the judge's bench, the choir as the jury box, the atrium as the witness stand, the balustrade separating the congregation, and the local authorities positioned before it." Chase (2014), p. 165.

[25] Noticing this type of approach, Laércio Becker points out: "the grandeur, the standardized colors, the ceremonial robes present in processions and forensic rituals (…) it is interesting to observe the zeal with which the legislator tends to regulate this seemingly irrelevant matter in the forensic sphere. Appellate judges wore ceremonial robes, capes, and caps (…) in colonial Brazil, a Royal Decree of 04/09/1600 ordered that judges wear robes, and a Royal Decree of 06/30/1652 established that they should wear the garnacha. During the Empire, Notice No. 447 of 01/05/1837 expressly established that they could not act while wearing tailcoats. Not even the justice of the peace escaped the regulation of attire (…) what is evident in all this regulation is, basically, the following: ritual and attire are used as barriers to *access to speech*. That is, they not only filter the layperson's access but also condition the very professional practice of legal practitioners." Becker (2012), pp. 146–147.

A first example of this type of approach can be identified in the study of "action" and the role it plays within the field of procedural law. As noted by Tarello, this topic has historically been among the most extensively studied by legal doctrine.[26] Surrounding it are debates of various kinds, granting this concept a central role in our theoretical framework.

It is based on this premise that, when consulting introductory works on civil procedure, the student will likely encounter the exposition of Celso's thought[27] and of the civil law theorists who gave it a new form.[28] Subsequently, they will find a few passages dedicated to the "controversy" between Windscheid and Muther,[29] as well as theoretical frameworks such as those of Wach[30] or Couture.[31] Finally, they will certainly examine in detail the perspective of Chiovenda[32] and the "eclectic theory" developed by Liebman.[33]

Thus, it becomes evident that understanding the concept of action involves a rather sophisticated theoretical framework, encompassing various paths and developments. In this context, the main point to be raised here is that, critically, the substance of this guarantee is also subject to different readings and interpretations. In other words, it is necessary to carefully consider any attempt to dogmatize it by treating it as a static criterion guiding civil procedure.

---

[26] Thus, presenting Tarello's notion on the subject and already warning against the risks of idealism, see Tarello (1989).

[27] According to the version that has reached the present day, the definition by Celso, long adopted in legal doctrine, held that "*actio autem nihil aliud est, quam ius persequendi in iudicio quod sibi debetur.*" (that is, "an action is the right of an individual to seek in court what is owed to them").

[28] Explaining this logic, Couture notes that "for this tendency, action is law in motion; it is nothing other than a dynamic possibility of law; a kind of capacity for exercise that is inherent to law itself (…) using an image that is more poetic than legal, it has been said that 'law dons its helmet and prepares for war.' Action and law are one and the same, within an apparent duality. A right would cease to be such if it did not contain action within it. The law that speaks of 'rights and actions,' as Demolombe said, is guilty of pleonasm." Couture (1942), pp. 18–19.

[29] On this subject, summarizing the debate between Windscheid and Muther, see Windscheid and Muther (1974).

[30] The issue is discussed in Chiovenda (1993), pp. 11–13.

[31] It should be noted that, as Marinoni, Arenhart, and Mitidiero state, this approach taken by the author can only be observed in the most recent editions of his *Fundamentos del derecho procesal civil*, differing from the position adopted in the first edition of the work, in which Couture asserted that "la acción, poder jurídico dirigido a obtener la actividad de la jurisdicción, tiene un conjunto de características particulares que la hacen diferir claramente de la simple petición a la autoridad" ("the action, a legal power aimed at obtaining the activity of the judiciary, has a set of particular characteristics that clearly distinguish it from a mere petition to the authority"). See Marinoni et al. (2015), p. 199. Couture (1942), p. 33.

[32] "Action is a power *before* the adversary rather than *against* the adversary (…) Action is a power in the face of which the adversary is not bound to anything: for if the action protects a subjective right, the obligation to satisfy the protected subjective right remains, as before, its content (…) Nor does any procedural duty of the adversary correspond to the action: there is simply and solely his subjection to the legal effects sought by the action. These legal effects (…) are the implementation of the law." Chiovenda (1993), p. 15.

[33] For an exposition on the understanding of this topic, see Liebman (1962), pp. 22–53.

In the same way, this risk of conceptualism is also inherent in the position attributed to the idea of "jurisdiction" within the proceedings. Here too, there is a constant danger that the notion may become a *dogma*, resulting in an artificial understanding of the subject.

Thus, in traditional literature, it is common for the study of the subject to begin with the presentation of the theories of Chiovenda,[34] Carnelutti,[35] and Allorio[36]—each, in its own way, reflecting the construction of a procedural system aligned with the liberal context. Similarly, ideas are presented that begin to relate *jurisdiction* to more effective substantive protection,[37] or to the very unity of the judicial system itself.[38] Additionally, notions such as the social and political purposes of procedure are revisited,[39] viewing it also as a means for promoting structural reforms.[40]

In any case, the point to be noted here is the same: the analysis of civil procedure, no matter how much it cannot dispense with concepts, must constantly ensure that their use is properly balanced. It is necessary to guarantee that the understanding of the subject is not constrained by classical interpretations and constructions as

[34] "Jurisdiction consists in the application of the law through the substitution of the activity of public bodies for that of private individuals, either by affirming the existence of a will of the law or by subsequently putting it into practice." Chiovenda (1922), p. 349.

[35] Although Carnelutti is generally credited exclusively with the understanding of jurisdiction as the "just resolution of a conflict of legally protected interests (dispute)," there is a notable shift in his approach in the work *Diritto e Processo*. This change is justified by the fact that the initial concept ("just resolution of the dispute") does not encompass cases of voluntary jurisdiction. In this context, Carnelutti adapts his previous construction—without discarding it for contentious jurisdiction—to conceive the purpose of the judicial process as the "fulfillment of the law." See Carnelutti (1958), pp. 40–66.

[36] For Allorio's position on the matter, see, among others, Allorio (1963).

[37] In Denti's words, "one can, therefore, reach the conclusion that, once the right of action is elevated to a constitutional guarantee—which places it outside the concrete regulation of procedure—the power to initiate proceedings can be more accurately defined as the power to file a legal claim, or simply the power of claim *tout court* ." Denti (1989), p. 116.

[38] In identifying the origin of the issue, the authors observe that "the shift in the concept of interpretation, the strength of constitutionalism, and judicial activity through the concretization of open-ended rules have given rise to a model of judge entirely different from that desired by the Romano-Canonical tradition." They further note that "in countries that did not need to entertain the absurd notion that judges could not interpret the law, it was naturally accepted that legal certainty and predictability would have to be sought elsewhere. And where was that? Precisely in precedents or, more specifically, in *stare decisis* ." Marinoni et al. (2015), pp. 144–145.

[39] See Calamandrei (1950). Also, Dinamarco (1987).

[40] In the words of Fiss, "adjudication is the process by which the values embodied in an authoritative legal text, such as the Constitution, are given concrete meaning and expression (...) but in the civil rights era a new form of adjudication emerged. This new form of adjudication is largely defined by two characteristics. The first is the awareness that the basic threat to our constitutional values is posed not by individuals but by the operations of large-scale organizations (...) Second, this new model of litigation reflects the realization that, unless the organizations that threaten these values are restructured, these threats to constitutional values cannot and will not be eliminated." Fiss (1979).

insurmountable restraints, but rather to critically recognize their flexibility and cultural context.[41]

- The indicated risk, therefore, lies in the use of broad conceptual formulas as a means to legitimize any procedural action—even without a precise understanding of the meaning of these formulas. For example, it is possible to assert that a particular procedure is appropriate because it consolidates "due process." However, this would be a purely rhetorical (and therefore fragile) legitimization if one does not actually understand what "due process" entails.

In this regard, it is essential to avoid an excessive gap between theory and practice, ensuring ongoing dialogue between the two. For example, although it is common to approach the subject from a "general theory" perspective (encompassing both civil and criminal procedure[42]), we consider it advisable to temper such

[41] After all, as observed by Calmon de Passos, "there is no ideal, model, or archetypal Law whose realization we are striving for. There is a legal system within which we operate and with which we are in tune. All law is socially constructed, historically formulated, and responds to the contingencies and circumstances of the time and place in which political power operates, as well as to the correlation of forces effectively opposed within the society in which that power has become institutionalized." Passos (2000), p. 52.

[42] Explaining the issue, Ada Pellegrini Grinover states that "studies on constitutional procedure have created a methodological environment for the development of a general theory of procedure, since it is in the Constitution, above all, that one finds the common platform for the various procedural disciplines. In Brazil, we have already had João Mendes Jr. and José Frederico Marques as forerunners of the view that there are major principles common to both civil and criminal procedure. The renewed interest in constitutional procedural law, as a method for defining the major concepts and structures of the system, has, in the same vein, led to a renewed interest in the general theory of procedure, which brings together general principles common to the various branches of procedural law, in a critical and unified perspective capable of introducing the study of the different procedural disciplines." Along the same lines, Dinamarco states that "the general theory of procedure is, from this perspective, a system of concepts and principles elevated to the highest degree of useful generalization and inductively condensed from the comparison of the various branches of procedural law. It transcends procedural dogmatics, as it is not concerned with the inquiry or formulation of rules or norms of positive law. For this reason, it tends toward universalization, overcoming the spatial and temporal limitations of positive law." Grinover (1993), p. 281. Dinamarco (1987), pp. 75–76.

ambitions. The functional differences between these fields can render generalization problematic,[43] increasingly justifying a conjectural observation of the discipline.[44]

In short, to critically understand the judicial process, it is necessary to prevent purely theoretical aspects from appearing natural, thereby establishing a constant bridge between the analysis of the discipline and its concrete needs. In other words, it is essential to bring the procedural system found in books closer to the procedural system as it occurs in reality, ensuring that both move forward in step with one another.

To enable this approach, each debate concerning procedural institutions should give rise to a new set of questions: Is there a real possibility that this discourse will be materially beneficial? Is there harmony between the theoretical argument and the context in which it is situated? How can the discussion contribute on a substantive level?

If at another time these questions might have been relegated to the background, we believe that today they constitute a fundamental issue. Only in this way is it possible to prevent the judicial process from resembling an architectural project that is captivating on paper, but impractical and riddled with blind spots.

[43] The functional difference between the two state functions is, in fact, already recognized by Carnelutti himself, who, when analyzing the subject, notes: "Cognition is necessary to enforce both the restitutive sanction and the penal sanction: how could one take something from someone to give it to another, or imprison someone, without being certain that he stole it? But there is a fundamental difference between the two cases. The question of whether the item should be returned involves a conflict of interests between two parties, the alleged thief and the alleged victim: if it is returned, the latter benefits and the former suffers; if it is not returned, the opposite occurs. Whether or not the alleged thief is imprisoned, however, does not create a similar conflict; it may appear so, but such an appearance is a superstition. It is important to note immediately that it is a superstition (…) the truth is, on the one hand, that society's interest lies solely in punishment if the person is guilty, not if he is innocent; on the contrary, punishing an innocent person would itself be a disorder, harming society's interests; there is, therefore, an essential difference between society's interest in punishing the alleged thief and the alleged victim's interest in the restitution of the item." In turn, Jacinto Nelson de Miranda Coutinho problematizes the issue, stating that "what is certain, in summary, is that the conflict of interests that may exist is not sufficient to encompass the content of criminal proceedings in all their forms and stages," and, from this, concludes that "the dispute, in any of its forms, is unacceptable in criminal proceedings; that is, to refer to the content of criminal proceedings, neither the civil nor the criminal dispute suffices (…) the content of the proceedings can be described by the expression 'criminal case.'" Thus, Carnelutti (1958), pp. 47–48. Coutinho (1989), pp. 134–149.

[44] "Although tradition may legitimize the use of the expression 'general theory of procedure' in certain contexts for better communication with the academic community, it is clear that there are *functional differences* between civil procedure and criminal procedure—not to mention the differences between judicial and non-judicial proceedings—that preclude their joint theorization. As these functional differences are reflected in the *main features* of civil procedure, in the *formulation of its concepts*, and in the *structuring of the procedure* as a whole, the ideal is for civil procedure to be theorized autonomously." Marinoni et al. (2015), pp. 23–24.

- In this context, aspects such as the judicial protection of vulnerable parties[45] and the concrete possibilities of access to judicial relief[46] come into play. Investigations into the power relations that influence the field[47] or the proportionality of its instruments[48] also gain particular importance. It becomes necessary to establish a constant link between theoretical discourse and reality, recognizing this adjustment as an essential point of observation.

In summary, it is up to the scholar to tie these threads together, bringing the objective and the subjective closer and avoiding purely rationalist elements. This observation is traditional in the field of epistemology.[49] Only in this way can the

[45] "Even in the administration of justice there is a real danger that the poor man will find himself at the same disadvantage that is his lot wherever the democratic system protects only his political and civil liberties, which are the common possessions of all citizens. For the man who lacks the economic means necessary for making these liberties a reality, they are often nothing but an unfilled promise. 'The law is the same for all' is a beautiful sentiment that warms the heart of the poor man when he sees it written on the wall of the courtroom, high over the heads of the judges, but when he discovers that to avail himself of his presumed equality he must spend more money than he can afford, the beautiful phrase becomes a sour jest, as if he had read on the wall that by virtue of the constitutional provision for freedom of the press (Art. 21) all citizens are equally free to publish a newspaper of large circulation, or that by virtue of the provision granting freedom of education (Art. 34) all citizens are equally free to send their children to a university." Calamandrei (1956), pp. 89–90.

[46] In this regard, Cappelletti and Garth (1988). See also Mancuso (2011).

[47] In this regard, Chiarloni (1975), p. 20 et seq. See also Passos (2000). See also Silva (2004).

[48] See, among others, Caponi (2011) pp. 399–415. See also Arenhart (2013).

[49] As an example, it is possible to establish, based on Durkheim's thought, that "at the moment when a new order of phenomena becomes the object of science, they are already represented in the mind, not only by sensory images, but by roughly formed kinds of concepts (…) man cannot live among things without forming ideas about them, according to which he regulates his conduct. It so happens that, since these notions are closer to us and more accessible than the realities to which they correspond, we naturally tend to substitute the latter for the former and to make them the very substance of our speculations. Instead of observing things, describing them, and comparing them, we are content to become aware of our ideas, to analyze them, to combine them. Instead of a science of realities, we do nothing more than an ideological analysis (…) this proceeds from ideas to things, not from things to ideas. It is clear that this method could not yield objective results." Delving into the issue, it is evident that, in the author's view, "social facts" would be the object of sociology, and it would not be viable to replace them with concepts, thus requiring the relativization of these tools. In other words, the study must constantly reside in the (externalized) facts, and not in the ideas and preconceptions related to them. Similarly, this deconstruction of the absolute value of concepts and the problematic reconciliation between objectivity and subjectivity are also present in Weber's thought. Thus, the theorist proposes the constant pursuit of value neutrality, requiring the scientist (insofar as possible) to challenge their own values. It is also in this context that the technique of "ideal types" assumes renewed importance. Given the unattainability of strict objectivity, these generalizations—filtered through subjectivity but forged from reality—are the data capable of reducing the fluidity and infinity of everyday life. In summary, it is necessary to reach the objective element in order to avoid the cognitive distortion resulting from the overvaluation of concepts. On this point, see Durkheim (2007), pp. 15–16; Becker (2007), p. 145; Serbena (2010); Weber (1989), pp. 125–126.

discipline remain connected to the world of facts, absorbing the complexity that surrounds it.

3.3 Reasons to Question the Judicial Process

In closing this chapter, we believe that its course leads us to yet another recommendation. Briefly put, if civil procedure faces two risks—concepts and rituals—that may distance it from concrete needs, it is necessary to subject them to constant scrutiny. We must question the procedural system, acknowledging its artificial nature and recognizing the possibility of its deconstruction.

Thus, we argue that it is important to bring a more skeptical mindset to the discipline, preventing its study from being limited to a purely credulous approach. Raising questions about the certainties that exist in its field and recognizing the possibility that any absolute statement may be unfounded; ultimately, breaking the image of naturalness that characterizes its current configuration and acknowledging its illusory condition.[50]

To describe this behavior, it is valuable to draw on the thought of Richard Posner. In order to construct his pragmatic reading of the legal sphere, the theorist expressly states that he adopts a skeptical approach, as a perspective rather than as a theory[51]. In his words, "*[M]y own skepticism is a mood or attitude—a disposition to scoff at pretensions to certainty, to question claims (even my own) (…) and to disbelieve in absolutes and unobservable entities—rather than a theory.*"[52] This is precisely the approach we wish to bring to civil procedure, introducing a more *critical* perspective in its assessment.

Based on this premise, the intention is not to discourage the development of theories related to the discipline, nor to deny that one of them may be contingently more appropriate. On the contrary, what we consider essential is that, in this discourse, greater caution is exercised regarding everything that appears to be *obvious* or *evident*—requiring a continuous alignment between premises and findings.

- This type of reasoning is illustratively exemplified by Posner: "*[I]f a clock is not working, it must be repaired. In this example, the 'must be' arises from two observations: the clock is not working, and the function of the clock is to tell*

[50] In Bourdieu's words, "the sociologist will never be able to put an end to spontaneous sociology and must impose upon himself an incessant polemic against the blinding evidence that, with little effort, provides the illusion of immediate knowledge and its unsurpassable richness. His difficulty in establishing, between perception and science, the separation that, for the physicist, is expressed by a clear opposition between the laboratory and everyday life, is all the greater because he cannot find, in his theoretical heritage, the tools that would allow him to radically reject ordinary language and common notions." From this, it follows that the fact must be conquered, constructed, and verified. Bourdieu (2002), p. 23.

[51] Posner (1988), p. 829.

[52] Posner (1988), p. 829.

time."[53] Thus, if one were to argue that the clock has become merely decorative, the conclusion could also be different.

In short, approaching civil procedure from this perspective allows for a critical examination of its supposedly natural arguments, bringing the discipline into a field more conducive to inquiry. After all, what is civil procedure? What are its objectives and possibilities? Are there objective or theoretical limits to the discipline? How does this impact its guarantees and its functioning?

Delving deeper into this point, it is worth recalling that the contrast between the primacy of the question and the primacy of certainty is not a recent development in legal studies, having underpinned the well-known distinction between dogmatic and zetetic analyses.[54] On one hand, there is a perspective that privileges doubt, making it its central focus. On the other hand, there is an approach grounded in convictions, based on the assumption that certain premises are not open to questioning.

Beginning the analysis with the first of the points, the zetetic, we can establish that this approach is primarily investigative, placing emphasis on a critical perspective. As a central feature, there would be a continuous sense of estrangement, causing any aspect inherent to Law to be viewed with a questioning eye.[55] The search for stability would not be among the scholar's priorities, leading to speculation that tends toward the infinite.[56]

In turn, the *dogmatic* approach would have a different composition, starting from certain premises without subjecting them to critical examination. Even if only

[53] "If a watch is not working, it ought to be fixed. In this example the 'ought' is derived from two 'is's': that the watch is not working, and that the function of a watch is to tell time." Posner (1990), p. 352.

[54] The typology was originally outlined by Viehweg and has since played an important role in the study of Law. Explaining its main features, Tércio Sampaio Ferraz highlighted: "We therefore have two possibilities for investigating a problem: either by emphasizing the question aspect, or by emphasizing the answer aspect. If the question aspect is emphasized, the basic concepts, premises, and principles remain open to doubt. That is, those elements that form the basis for organizing a system of statements which, as a theory, explains a phenomenon, retain their hypothetical and problematic character (…) In the second aspect, by contrast, certain elements are, from the outset, removed from doubt, with the answer side prevailing. That is, placed beyond question and maintained as unassailable solutions, they are, at least temporarily, assumed to be irreplaceable (…) In the first case, using Viehweg's terminology, we have a zetetic approach; in the second, a dogmatic approach." Viehweg (1997). Ferraz Jr. (2001), pp. 40–41.

[55] The term is introduced by Carlo Ginzburg to highlight an attitude of *estrangement*, breaking the apathy inherent to everyday life. In the author's work, its use has a particularly *transcultural* emphasis, underscoring the importance of adopting a reflective perspective when considering aspects that are different from our own—which, for that reason, could be readily criticized. See Ginzburg (2001).

[56] In the words of Roesler, from the adoption of a zetetic perspective, "continuous reflexivity, which can call into question all the answers provided in the investigation (and for this reason, relevance is given to the aspect of questioning) points to an infinite process, or at least one without a defined end. In zetetic inquiry, therefore, answers are always regarded as attempts, provisional and subject to questioning at any moment, and their task is to characterize the horizon of questions within the chosen field." Roesler (2003), pp. 3–4.

superficially, these aspects would be tacitly accepted and removed from scrutiny. Likewise, since they are excluded from debate, these topics would not require further justification or explanation. Their assertion would be presumed, thereby influencing the actors involved.[57]

Given this context, it is not surprising that civil procedure has historically been associated with the second group. In general terms, only in this way would the fulfillment of its *guiding* function be ensured, of the order of *ought-to-be* that characterizes its practical domain.[58]

- As an example, when filing an appeal against a particular decision, it is clear that the party must comply with the legal deadline, disregarding any personal reservations in this regard. Similarly, when specifying the evidence they intend to present, the party must adhere to the applicable parameters, demonstrating a posture of compliance.

However, in this context, the discipline could move precisely toward dangers such as ritualism and conceptualism. By establishing immutable parameters and removing them from scrutiny, the subject matter could become detached from its own social environment.[59] Using the same examples, even though the deadline for an appeal or the criteria for specifying evidence must be respected today, they cannot be regarded as natural or exempt from theoretical objections.

In light of this blind spot, the attempt to bring civil procedure into a field more conducive to questioning is once again justified. In summary, although its actors must observe certain rules and set aside uncertainties regarding their application, this cannot blind them to social changes and needs. Without hindering its practical operation, the aim is to offer scholars a more critical perspective for reflection.

---

[57] "One can say, he asserts, that statements are treated as dogmata when, in principle, they are excluded in the long term from attack and, therefore, are not subject to any duty of defense, that is, to any duty of justification, but simply to a duty of explanation. In a given cultural context, certain statements are placed beyond all doubt." Idem. Roesler (2003), pp. 3–4.

[58] Expounding on this guiding directive, inherent to dogmatic discourse, Tercio Sampaio Ferraz Jr. states that "the dogmatic approach highlights the act of forming opinions and preserves some of those opinions. The zetetic approach, on the contrary, disintegrates and dissolves opinions, casting them into doubt. Zetetic questions have an explicit speculative function and are infinite. Dogmatic questions have an explicit directive function and are finite. In the former, the issue at hand is framed as a *being* (what is something?). In the latter, the situation is understood as an *ought-to-be* (how should something be?). Therefore, the zetetic approach seeks to know what a thing is. The dogmatic approach, in turn, is concerned with enabling a decision and guiding action." Ferraz Jr. (2001), p. 41.

[59] "The dogmatic study of law is linked to a double abstraction. That is, since there is no society without dogmas—because without fixed points of reference, social communication (human interaction) is impossible—every community develops its own norms. However, norms alone are not sufficient; they also require rules of interpretation. Thus, we have an abstract product, the rules, whose object is another abstract product, the norms. Hence the double abstraction. As a result, its study pays a price: the risk of a progressive distancing from social reality itself." Ferraz Jr. (2001), p. 49.

References

Allorio, E. (1963). *Problemas de Derecho Procesal*. EJEA.

Arenhart, S. C. (2013). *A tutela coletiva de interesses individuais: para além da proteção dos interesses individuais homogêneos*. Ed. RT.

Auerbach, J. S. (2007). Justiça sem Direito. In A. G. De Azevedo & I. M. Barbosa (Eds.), *Estudos em Arbitragem, Mediação e Negociação*. Universidade de Brasília.

Becker, H. S. (2007). *Segredos e Truques da Pesquisa*. Zahar.

Becker, L. A. (2012). Erosão do Sagrado Processual. In L. A. Becker (Ed.), *Qual é o jogo do processo?* Sérgio Fabris.

Bourdieu, P. (1989). *O Poder Simbólico*. Difusão Editorial.

Bourdieu, P. (2002). *A Profissão de Sociólogo* (3rd ed.). Editora Vozes.

Bush, R. A., & Folger, J. (2005). *The promise of mediation – The transformative approach to conflict*. John Wiley & Sons.

Calamandrei, P. (1956). *Procedure and democracy*. New York University Press.

Calamandrei, P. (1950). Processo e Giustizia. *Rivista di Diritto Processuale, 5*.

Caponi, R. (2011). O princípio da proporcionalidade na justiça civil. *Revista de Processo, 192*.

Cappelletti, M., & Garth, B. (1988). *Acesso à justiça*. Sérgio Fabris.

Carnelutti, F. (1958). *Diritto e Processo*. Morano Editore.

Chase, O. G. (2014). *Direito, Cultura e Ritual*. Editora Marcial Pons.

Chiarloni, S. (1975). *Introduzione allo studio del diritto processuale*. G. Giappichelli.

Chiovenda, G. (1993). L'azioni nel sistema dei diritti. In G. Chiovenda (Ed.), *Saggi di Diritto Processuale Civile* (Vol. 1). Giuffrè.

Chiovenda, G. (1922). *Principios de Derecho Procesal*. Editorial Réus.

Coutinho, J. N. M. (1989). *A lide e o conteúdo do processo penal*. Juruá.

Couture, E. J. (1942). *Fundamentos del Derecho Procesal Civil*. Aniceto Lopez Editor.

Damaška, M. (1986). *The faces of justice and state authority*. Yale University Press.

Denti, V. (1989). *La giustizia civile – Lezioni introduttive*. Il Mulino.

Dinamarco, C. R. (1987). *A instrumentalidade do processo*. Ed. RT.

Durkheim, E. (2007). *As regras do método sociológico*. Martins Fontes.

Edwards, T. (2007). *Cultural theory: Classical and contemporary positions*. Sage.

Evans-Pritchard, E. E. (1976). *Withcraft, Oracles, and Magic among the Azande*. Oxford University Press.

Ferraz, T. S., Jr. (2001). *Introdução ao estudo do direito: técnica, dominação e decisão* (3rd ed.). Atlas.

Fiss, O. (1979). The forms of justice. *Harvard Law Review, 93*.

Geertz, C. (1973). *The interpretation of cultures*. Basic Books.

Gilley, B. (2006). The meaning and measure of state legitimacy: Results for 72 countries. *European Journal of Political Research, 45*.

Ginzburg, C. (2001). *Olhos de madeira – novas reflexões sobre a distância*. São Paulo, Companhia das Letras.

Grinover, A. P. (1993). Modernidade do Direito Processual Civil Brasileiro. *Revista da Faculdade de Direito, 88*.

Hart, H. L. A. (1988). *The concept of law*. Oxford University Press.

Hodges, C. (2008). *The reform of class and representative actions in European legal systems*. Hart Publishing.

Lacerda, G. (1961). Processo e Cultura. *Revista de Direito Processual Civil, 3*.

Liebman, E. T. (1962). L'azione nella teoria del processo civile. In E. T. Liebman (Ed.), *Problemi del Processo Civile*. Morano.

Mancuso, R. C. (2011). *Acesso à justiça: condicionantes legítimas e ilegítimas*. Ed. RT.

Marinoni, L. G., Arenhart, S. C., & Mitidiero, D. (2015). *Novo Curso de Processo Civil – Tutela dos Direitos Mediante Procedimentos Diferenciados*. Ed. RT.

Minkov, M. (2012). *Cross-cultural analysis: The science and art of comparing world's modern societies and their cultures*. Sage.
Mitidiero, D. (2004). Processo e Cultura: Praxismo, Processualismo e Formalismo em Direito Processual Civil. *Genesis: Revista de Direito Processual Civil, 33*.
Muller, A. (2005). *Concepts of culture – art, politics & society*. University of Calgary Press.
Passos, J. J. C. (2000). *Direito, poder, justiça e processo: julgando os que nos julgam*. Forense.
Posner, R. A. (1990). *The problems of jurisprudence*. Harvard University Press.
Posner, R. A. (1988). The jurisprudence of skepticism. *Michigan Law Review, 86*.
Roesler, C. R. (2003). Enfoque dogmático e enfoque zetético como pontos de partida para realizar a interdisciplinaridade no Ensino Jurídico Contemporâneo. *Revista Eletrônica de Direito Educacional, 4*.
Sacco, R. (2001). *Introdução ao direito comparado*. Ed. RT.
Serbena, C. A. (2010). Objetividade e subjetividade nas ciências jurídicas e sociais: Durkheim e Weber. *Revista da Faculdade de Direito de Uberlândia, 38*.
Silva, O. A. B. (2004). *Processo e Ideologia: o Paradigma Racionalista*. Forense.
Soares, C. H. (2012). Estudo sistemático do direito processual civil chileno. *Revista de Processo, 223*.
Stürner, R., & Kern, C. (2011). Processo civil comparado – Tendências recentes e fundamentais. *Revista de Processo, 200*.
Suarez, C. D. (2013). O panorama atual e a problemática procedimental em torno da tutela inibitória. *Revista de Processo, 226*.
Tamanaha, B. Z. (2009). A concise guide to the rule of law. In G. Palombella & N. Walker (Eds.), *Relocating the rule of law*. Hart Publishing.
Tarello, G. (1989). Quattro buoni giuristi per una cattiva azione. In G. Tarello (Ed.), *Dottrine del processo civile: studi storici sulla formazione del diritto processuale civile*. Il Mulino.
Taruffo, M. (2009). Cultura e Processo. *Rivista Trimestrale di Diritto e Procedura Civile, LXIII*.
Torrano, B. (2014). *Do fato à legalidade: introdução à teoria analítica do direito*. Lumen Juris.
Viehweg, T. (1997). Problemas Sistémicos en la Dogmática Jurídica y en la Investigación Jurídica. In T. Viehweg (Ed.), *Tópica y filosofía del derecho* (2nd ed.). Gedisa.
Weber, M. (1989). A "objetividade" do conhecimento nas ciências sociais. In G. Cohn (Ed.), *Max Weber* (3rd ed.). Editora Ática.
Windscheid, B., & Muther, T. (1974). *Polemica sobre la "actio"*. EJEA.

Chapter 4
How to Critically Analyze Civil Procedure?

4.1 The Real Limits of Civil Procedure

In the previous chapter, we saw that critically analyzing civil procedure is essential to foster a closer connection between its theoretical framework and practical reality. Only in this way can the discipline be grounded more concretely, preventing an undesirable divergence between theory and practice.

Against this backdrop, from this point onward, we aim to present some elements that may contribute to this approach. The first concerns the existence of substantive limits inherent to the discipline, which are not always recognized by its classical theory. At least two central points are included here: (i) the costs of the judicial process in a context of scarcity; and (ii) the possibility of failure in its response.

To address the initial aspect, we remind the reader that dispute resolution, over time, has become a matter of State, thus framing it within civil procedure. Accordingly, an essential point of support emerges for the development of this subject: if the public sphere suffers from resource scarcity, procedural institutions will also be affected by this issue.

- In other words, by combining theoretical works and practical reality, we realize that it is impossible to seriously consider the discipline without taking into account its costs and possibilities. Each debate on the subject thus gives rise to a new set of questions: when discussing electronic hearings, are we proposing something compatible with the public budget? Can we advocate for an increase in the possibilities for appeal without considering its impact on the organization of the courts?

By raising this type of question, we introduce into civil procedure a broader issue that has prompted various debates. This concerns the question of the costs of rights. The topic was notably addressed by Holmes and by Sunstein, demonstrating that there is an element here that must be considered in the structure of any legal system.

G. Osna, *Civil Procedure, Culture, and Proportionality*,
https://doi.org/10.1007/978-3-032-27555-4_4

To understand this element, let us consider the following analogy: on one hand, "A" is the owner of a certain rural property and carries out agricultural activities on it. On the other hand, "B" undergoes periodic radiotherapy sessions at a public hospital located in the same region. Although these two situations are distinct, they share a common aspect: in both cases, a certain right guaranteed by our current legal system is being exercised. In one case, the fundamental right to property is at play. In the other, the fundamental right to health is at play.

Analyzing the issue in detail, we observe that the nature of each of these interests is quite distinct, with no overlap in the set of positions underlying them.[1] Employing the classical segmentation of rights into dimensions, one would be faced with an interest typically included in the first group and another that faithfully represents the second. Thus, while property has historically been viewed as a negative liberty, the protection of health would represent a step toward welfare and greater social provision.[2] From this difference arises a question: Is it appropriate to assert that only the protection of this second aspect would depend on state expenditures and efforts?

The intuitive response might be affirmative, arguing that the full protection of first-generation interests would not necessarily entail significant expenditures.

It is at this point, however, that Holmes and Sunstein introduce a new element to the discussion, arguing that there is no right without inherent costs associated with its enforcement. This is because, even in cases where the guarantee appears to be negative, the State is obliged to oversee its implementation and to address any violations or distortions.[3] This conclusion demystifies the belief in the exclusively abstentionist nature of "liberty rights," including property rights. Here as well,

[1] Alexy observes that "when one speaks of a fundamental right, for example, to life or to freedom of expression, one generally refers not only to individual positions but to the fundamental right as a whole. What is a fundamental right as a whole? The simplest answer is that a fundamental right as a whole is a bundle of fundamental legal positions. The question remains as to what unites the various individual fundamental legal positions into a fundamental right." Based on this, the author recognizes the dynamic nature of such interests, conceiving them as principles and noting their susceptibility to balancing. Alexy (1993), p. 241.

[2] Identifying this issue, Ingo Sarlet states that the interests included in the first group are generally "presented as rights of a 'negative' nature, since they require abstention rather than positive action on the part of public authorities, and are, in this sense, 'rights of resistance or opposition vis-à-vis the State.' Of particular importance among these rights, especially due to their well-known natural law inspiration, are the rights to life, liberty, property, and equality before the law." On the other hand, with regard to the second category, he emphasizes that "the distinguishing feature of these rights is their positive dimension, since they are no longer concerned with preventing State intervention in the sphere of individual liberty, but rather, in the precise formulation of C. Lafer, with providing a 'right to participate in social welfare.' Thus, it is no longer a matter of freedom from and before the State, but rather freedom through the State. These fundamental rights (…) are still characterized today by granting individuals entitlements to state social benefits, such as social assistance, health, and education." Thus, Sarlet (2009), p. 47.

[3] "No right is simply a right to be left alone by public officials. All rights are claims to an affirmative governmental response (…) judicial accessibility and openness to appeal are crowning achievements of liberal state-building (…) to the extent that rights enforcement depends upon judicial vigilance, rights cost, at a minimum, whatever it costs to recruit, train, supply, pay, and (in turn) monitor the judicial custodians of our basic rights." Holmes and Sunstein (2000), pp. 44–45.

enforcement would require a certain degree of state action. In summary, every protected interest entails a cost, which must ultimately be borne by the taxpayer.

This theory has had a significant impact on legal scholarship,[4] giving renewed meaning to the notion of "tragic choices" in the budgetary context.[5] The governmental "blanket" is short, lacking sufficient reach to fully provide for all that is expected of it.[6] Decision-making in this sphere, therefore, will inevitably involve sacrifices and trade-offs.

As noted by Álvaro Perez Ragone, this impacts civil procedure, which operates under objective constraints imposed by limited resources.[7] Thus, even though the complexity of the subject matter might suggest that a judge should devote weeks to a single case, this is rarely feasible. Judicial activity is inevitably costly, which imposes limits on its scope.[8]

- This scenario introduces an important real-world component to the study of the subject. From the debate on the judge's investigative powers to the discussion on the scope of the adversarial principle, no argument can be effective without taking this point into account. To draw a brief analogy, there is no use in planning

---

[4] Thus, Amaral (2001). See also Galdino (2005).

[5] The term is coined by Calabresi and Bobbitt, who, in analyzing the decision-making process related to the allocation of budgetary resources, recognize that "the distribution of some goods entails great suffering or death. When attention is riveted on such distributions they arouse emotions of compassion, outrage, and terror. It is then that conflicts are laid bare between on the one hand, those values by which society determined the beneficiaries of the distributions, and (with nature) the perimeters of scarcity, and on the other hand, those humanistic moral values which prize life and well-being." Calabresi and Bobbit (1978), p. 18.

[6] "The short blanket metaphor is suitable for understanding any budget, but it is even more appropriate for grasping the limitations of the Brazilian public budget. It is an insufficient blanket to cover all parts of the body at the same time. If it covers the feet, the hands are left exposed to the elements. But if it covers the hands, it cannot cover the feet." Clève (2006), p. 36.

[7] "The longer or shorter duration of a given proceeding, the greater or lesser legitimacy of a judgment, is not, in itself, a matter of interest only to the parties. To speak today of 'the matters of the parties' vs. 'the matters of the judge' is to misunderstand the concept of due and fair process. There is not only a procedural due process clause with merely negative content: it is not permissible for the judiciary to intervene beyond what is appropriate in a given case (…) Indeed, the conduct of a judicial proceeding is of interest and concern to all citizens who, through their taxes, finance the justice system—even if they do not use it—and even more so to those whose rights, in need of protection, must be postponed from entering and perhaps being decided because current human and infrastructural resources are being allocated to other, earlier cases. Even though civil justice seeks to protect and resolve the disputes of the parties as individuals, the use of judicial resources does not seem to be solely a matter for the parties, or at least not exclusively for them." Ragone (2016).

[8] "The constitutional right to due process – like the private right to bring an action in contract or tort – presupposes that, at the taxpayer's expense, the state maintains and makes accessible complex and relatively transparent legal institutions within which the cumbersome formalities of fair, public, and understandable adjudication occur (…) giving citizens access to courts and other adjudicative forums is not like giving them access to natural harbors and navigable waters, because the government must not only brush aside hindrance to access, but must actually create the institutions to which access is being granted." Holmes and Sunstein (2000), pp. 53–54.

the construction of a grand building like the *Empire State* if the available materials and labor are not even sufficient to complete a ten-story building. The same applies to the procedural machinery.

Alongside this aspect, another real barrier has also been noted above that must be recognized by scholars in the field: the fallible nature of its capacity to provide answers. Whether due to the bounded rationality of its agents or the interpretive openness of the normative text, it is impossible to understand dispute resolution without taking this obstacle into account. Concepts such as uncertainty and insecurity cannot be excluded from its lexicon.

To clarify this point, it is important to recall that civil procedure is fundamentally structured around *conflict*, seeking to resolve interests that are, in some way, opposed. In other words, when "A" and "B" disagree on a particular matter and submit its resolution to the judiciary, it is the role of the proceedings to provide an answer to the dispute. This means that the judge is constantly called upon to act in contentious matters, rendering decisions that favor one party and are unfavorable to the other.

Against this backdrop, it is impossible to understand civil procedural law without considering its constant need to choose between and discard conflicting arguments. In this context, the debate may be more or less complex, involving a more or less ambiguous cognitive process. Similarly, the discussion may focus on concrete events related to the dispute ("questions of fact") or on the legal treatment to be applied to them ("questions of law"). However, all these scenarios share a common feature: uncertainty regarding the answer.

In fact, considering that the state entity does not draft judgments or preside over hearings, its participation in court takes place through a citizen vested with judicial authority—a flesh-and-blood judge. It is the judge who will conduct and decide the case, ensuring that the dispute is always subject to limited rationality[9]. This is an

---

[9] Indeed, when analyzing this possibility of judicial cognition, it is valuable to recall that, in the field of behavioral analysis, the idea that human conduct is guided by the maximization of desired outcomes has already gained significant traction. However, this criterion is pursued within an environment of *limited* data and information (*bounded rationality*). Addressing this issue, Jones notes: "Do people make rational decisions in politics and economics? Not if by 'rational' we mean that they demonstrate conformity to the classic expected utility model. There is no longer any doubt about the weight of the scientific evidence; the expected-utility model of economic and political decision making is not sustainable empirically. From the laboratory comes failure after failure of rational expected utility to account for human behavior. From systematic observation in organizational settings, scant evidence of behavior based on the expected-utility model emerges. Does this mean that people (and therefore their politics) are irrational? Not at all. People making choices are intendedly rational. They want to make rational decisions, but they cannot always do so (…) In structured situations, at least, we may conceive of any decision as having two components: environmental demands (seen by the individual as incentives, positive or negative) and bounds on adaptability in the given decision-making situation. Ideally, an analysis based on rational choice should be able to specify what the environmental incentives are and to predict decisions based on those incentives. What cannot be explained is either random error (even the most rational of us may make an occasional mistake, but these are not systematic) or bounded rationality showing through." Thus, Jones (1999), pp. 297–298.

obstacle inherent to the human condition, which may be exacerbated by the precariousness of the judicial structure.[10] As noted by Posner, it is the judge's responsibility to decide personally, while undertaking the arduous task of realizing a greater interest.[11]

Based on this foundation, a first point to note is that it will always be possible for the judge to interpret the factual basis of a given case differently from what is socially expected, no matter how straightforward it may seem. In other words, even in the presence of clear evidence, there is a risk that its interpretation may encounter problems or limitations in understanding, leading the dispute to a conclusion quite different from what initially appeared most likely.[12]

---

[10] In addressing this issue, Mancuso points out that "the assumption, by the State-judge, of conflicts that have arisen and have not been resolved either autonomously or through third-party intervention between the interested parties or between them and the Public Administration, was not accompanied by an equal concern for the proper management of the immense volume of cases that began to accumulate in the judicial archives, both at the first and second instance levels. Nor was there any effective attention given to controlling the *effectiveness* of judicial services, disregarding the warning that *quantity ultimately affects quality* (…) as is said in the field of 'organization and method,' *those who desire the ends must provide the means*, and what is observed is that the Brazilian State chose to assume the monopoly of dispensing justice, but did not demonstrate commitment or proficiency in providing it with the human and material resources necessary to produce a high-quality final result." Mancuso (2014), pp. 58–59.

[11] "A related question is who a federal judge's principal is, or indeed whether there is one in a meaningful sense. Is it the judges of a highest court – but then who are the principals of the judges of the highest court? If the principals are not other judges, are they the members of Congress? The President who appointed the judges? The current President? The American people? The framers of the Constitution? The Constitution itself, or statutes and precedents? But can documents be principals? 'The law'? Whatever the answers, no society leaves its judges completely at large." Posner (2008), p. 126. In the same vein, see Sundfeld's teaching, emphasizing that "state activity is a function, subject to ends external to the agent. The legislator, the judge, the administrator, do not have the power to pursue their own interests or desires. Their acts are valid to the extent that they achieve the purposes assigned to them. Hence, it is said that the will of the State is functional. A punishment imposed on a civil servant for holding an ideology displeasing to the superior is void. It is inadmissible for a judge to dismiss a case because of a personal disagreement with the plaintiff. Public officials are merely channels for expressing the will of the law: the legislator, when enacting laws, expresses the will of the Constitution (and of the people); the judge and the administrator, through their acts, fulfill the will of the law." Sundfeld (2009), p. 92. Indeed, this creates a constant need for alignment, which is why Kornhauser points out that "economic models of judicial behavior and of court organization require an assumption concerning the motivations of judges. This requirement presents the central challenge to the economic analysis of courts." Kornhausen (2012), p. 310.

[12] It should be emphasized here that the discussion is not about a "false" or "true" conclusion, since the adequacy of this dichotomy is itself the subject of numerous controversies within the field of philosophy. Ranging from the contemporary pragmatism of Richard Rorty to the reinterpreted logic of adequacy by Susan Haack, the debate is intense and demonstrates that, in the procedural field, speaking of truth is (at the very least) problematic. This is why the option is to confront the decision with the expectations related to it, rather than with any metaphysically correct conclusion. In this regard, when summarizing his idea and his disbelief in any notion of "truth" (privileging "justification"), Rorty emphasized that "what was needed, and what the idealists were unable to envisage, was a repudiation of the very idea of anything - mind or matter, self or world - having an

- To illustrate this point, let us suppose that "A" files a claim for damages against "B," seeking compensation for losses suffered in a car accident. In this scenario, imagine that the plaintiff asserts that their vehicle was parked when it was struck by the defendant, presenting security camera footage to support the allegation and listing three witnesses who corroborate their account. In turn, let us suppose that "B" merely claims to have been with the vehicle in another city on the same date, and therefore, the accident could not have occurred.

  Even in an example as deliberately extreme as this, there are no guarantees regarding the outcome of the assessment. There will be constant uncertainty, with no way to fully ensure its predictability. This is a risk that becomes inherent to the debate.

Similarly, this uncertainty also plays a central role in the analysis and application of the legal rules relevant to the debate.[13] Here as well, factors such as bounded

---

intrinsic nature to be expressed or represented. For the idealists confused the idea that nothing has such a nature with the idea that space and time are unreal, that human beings cause the spatiotemporal world to exist. We need to make a distinction between the claim that the world is out there and the claim that truth is out there. To say that the world is out there, that it is not our creation, is to say, with common sense, that most things in space and time are the effects of causes which do not include human mental states. To say that truth is not out there is simply to say that where there are no sentences there is no truth, that sentences are elements of human languages, and that human languages are human creations. Truth cannot be out there - cannot exist independently of the human mind - because sentences cannot so exist, or be out there. The world is out there, but descriptions of the world are not. Only descriptions of the world can be true or false. The world on its own - unaided by the describing activities of human beings – cannot." On the other hand, it is worth mentioning Haack's words, taking the opposite view: "the concept of truth is internally related to the concepts of belief, evidence, and inquiry. To believe that p is to accept p as true. Evidence that p is evidence that p is true, an indication of the truth of p. And to inquire into whether p is to inquire into whether p is true; if you aren't trying to get the truth, you aren't really inquiring. (…) The genuine inquirer's love of truth, as this reveals, is not like the love of a collector for the antique furniture or exotic stamps he collects, nor is it like a religious person's love of God. He is not a collector of true propositions, nor is he a worshipper of an intellectual ideal. He is a person of intellectual integrity. He is not, like the fake reasoner, indifferent to the truth of the propositions for which he argues. He is not, like the sham reasoner, unbudgeably loyal to some proposition, committed however the evidence turns out. Whatever question he investigates, he tries to find the truth of that question, whatever the color of that truth may be." In the field of procedure, the issue can be exemplified by the recent debate between Taruffo and Cavallone, which presents two substantially different views on the subject, each grounded in distinct philosophical and epistemological foundations. See, on this point, Rorty (1993), p. 05; Haack (1996), pp. 57–59; Taruffo (2010), p. 995; Cavallone (2010), p. 01.

[13] Problematizing the issue, Bruno Torrano points out that "law is a system subject to the limitations inherent in the instruments its creators use to act in the world. Every written legal norm reflects the imperfections and confusions of thought characteristic of beings with limited rationality who inhabit an environment marked by resource scarcity and information asymmetry (…) if a norm is written, it is subject to the vagueness and imprecision inherent in language (…) the indeterminacies are not intentional, but are linked to the polysemy of the verbal meaning of the norm." Torrano (2014), p. 163.

rationality and hermeneutic plurality may lead to different outcomes,[14] allowing one to regard a decision as unjust or mistaken.[15]

- It is true that there are currently discourses seeking to mitigate this *uncertainty* by pursuing alternatives such as the standardization of case law through precedents. Nevertheless, we believe that even in this context, there will always be a constant risk of uncertainty. After all, to what extent does a given case resemble or differ from the rule established in the precedent? Is the very leading decision not itself open to interpretation? What degree of differentiation is required to justify a new judgment?

With these considerations, we do not intend to disregard the importance of the argument, but rather to emphasize that, even in this context, legal certainty does not possess as much assertiveness as one might wish.[16] Whether due to the interpretive

[14] Addressing this issue, Jerome Frank pointed out that "the problem is, in part, one of what today we call 'semantics.' Words serve as symbols. As such, necessarily they are somewhat compressed, condensed. Does the legislature's compression, which omits some particulars, indicate an intention to omit them? The judges must determine the proper limits of expansion of the condensed symbols. Judges often differ among themselves as to the appropriate amount of such expansion. The varieties of human experiences are legion. They cannot be dealt with mathematically. What, for instance, does the word 'value' or the word 'employees' mean when found in a statute? Were a legislature to try to tie down the courts by over-precise words, it would often defeat itself." Frank (1949), p. 294.

[15] Moreover, as noted by Schauer, the recognition of interpretive openness means that the same legal provision can be understood in substantially different ways by different actors. Addressing this issue, the author points out: "under what circumstances will which officials be given the freedom to exercise their own judgment and make their own choices, and under what circumstances will that freedom be constrained or even mostly eliminated? When a judge is determining which custody decision is in the best interests of the child, for example, she might be faced with a choice between a wealthy mother who can provide the child with high-quality education, housing, recreation, and culture and a less wealthy father who appears to understand the child better than the mother. Under these circumstances, some judges would prefer the mother and others the father, but the basic idea of discretion is that neither of these decisions, given the 'best interests of the child' standard, would be legally incorrect. People might criticize one or the other decision for being morally wrong, psychologically ignorant, or based on erroneous factual premises, and so it would not be correct to say that the two decisions are equally right. But it would be correct to say that the two decisions are equally legally right, and thus that either decision would, in the ordinary course of things, be upheld on appeal." Reinforcing this point, and drawing on Schauer's own thought, Bruno Torrano also observes that the opening of possible paths is a logical consequence of porosity, stating that "it is easy to imagine situations in which, despite the discussion involving a legally regulated situation, there is, on the one hand, excessive care in argumentation, but on the other, there continue to exist equally well-founded possible decisions that point in different directions. This is another central idea of discretion, which suggests that the term should be used in a broad sense: the complete and inevitable absence of reliable criteria to say that one of the possible decisions in a regulated case is legally incorrect." Schauer (2009), p. 190. Torrano (2014), p. 167.

[16] As Jerome Frank notes, "we must face the fact that judges are human. That should not dismay those of us who cherish democracy. For in a democracy it is a imperative never to forget that public offices are, of necessity, held by mere men, who, of course, have human foibles. It is only where government officials are deemed to be semi-divine that people have any excuse for ignoring the ineluctable personal factor in government. Wherefore the belief that government can ever consist of perfect creatures is alien to a democracy. That false belief constitutes the core of the philosophy

plurality inherent in any provision or the intrinsic limitations of all factual assessments, it is impossible to guarantee that the resolution of a dispute will follow the purportedly most appropriate course. This is an inevitable limitation and should be taken into account in the study of procedural law.

4.2 The Democratic Barriers of Civil Procedure

In this pursuit of aligning the dialogue between books and reality, we believe that a critical analysis of civil procedure brings yet another important contribution. In summary, as we saw in the previous chapter, there has been a recurring attempt to legitimize the subject through a "participatory" discourse. However, we contend that a critical analysis reveals blind spots in this assertion. In our view, Western civil procedure today is democratically limited. This is due both to its distinctly technical nature and to the imposition of a mandatory model of representation.

To approach this point, we find an important theoretical pillar in the thought of Mirjan Damaška, who relates two ideal types of state organization to two equally idealized methods of conflict resolution.[17] On one side is what the author refers to as the hierarchical process. On the other hand, there is the coordinate process. Although the framework is the same, the pictures painted are quite different, revealing that civil procedural law can assume distinct forms of management and administration.

Through this lens, we observe that the first of these models is premised on a clear distinction between professionals responsible for dispute resolution and other

---

of a dictatorship; it is the basis of 'personal government,' in its most extreme and pernicious form." In this sense, the presence of an element of *uncertainty* would be indelible in judicial activity. Frank (1949), p. 410.

[17] "Systematic study of features impressed on the legal process by state officialdom requires a scheme to identify and describe different modes of organizing procedural authority (...) hence I shall begin by developing a distinctive analytical framework. The conceptual elements needed for this framework correspond to three questions often asked in confronting an organization of authority; the first concerns the attributes of officials, the second, their relationship, and the third, the manner in which they make decisions. Thus separated out, these three aspects of authority have long been suspected of influencing the shape of the legal process, and I shall use them as dimensions along which to define our categories. On the first dimension, the usual focus is on the distinction between professionalized, permanent officials and those who are untrained and transitory. On the second dimension, two lesser configurations deserve special consideration: under the first, officials are locked into a strict network of super- and subordination; under the second, they are rough equals, organized into a single echelon of authority. On the third dimension, the critical distinction is between decision making pursuant to special or "technical" standards, and decision making informed by undifferentiated or general community norms. It is easy to see that these three larger aspects of authority are analytically independent, so that smaller variables from each dimension can be combined in various ways (...) but such extensive taxonomic exercises are not required: our theme permits selection of only two composite structures of authority." Damaška (1986), pp. 16–17.

citizens ("laypersons"),[18] organizing the Courts in a hierarchical manner and reinforcing their institutional unity.[19] This would establish a technocratic foundation, recommending that case resolution prioritize the use of pre-established statements, even if inattentive to material particularities.[20] All these aspects would reveal a considerable distance between the State and individuals, resulting in a structure characterized by greater centralization of power.[21]

At the other end of the spectrum, there would be a procedural framework that is also typified but guided by opposing values. This would be the coordinated process. Here, the barrier between the adjudicator and the rest of society would not exist,[22] allowing decisions to be based less on technical-legal parameters and more on the concrete needs related to the dispute.[23] Similarly, the judicial body would not require the same degree of hierarchy and review, resulting in greater internal parity.[24] The

[18] "Permanently placed officials carve out a sphere of practice which they regard as their special province. Over time, they also develop a sense of identity with similarly situated individuals, so that lines become rigid between 'insiders' and 'outsiders.' If outside participation in the making of decisions is imposed upon such officials, it is viewed, at best, as meddling which deserves to be contained and made innocuous." Damaška (1986), pp. 18–19.

[19] "This schism between office and its occupant promotes institutional thinking: impulses to bypass institutional interest and to consult one's conscience are too 'protestant' to be tolerated. Judgments become pronouncements of an impersonal entity (a curia) even where a single individual is entrusted with their rendition. And because the institution must be univocal so as not to be equivocal, the announcement of a judgment made by several officials nullifies prior internal dissent: those who disagree must now repress their feelings." Furthermore, "officials are organized into several echelons: power comes from the top, trickling down the levels of authority. Great inequalities among officials at different hierarchical positions are characteristic." Damaška (1986), p. 19.

[20] "Under this approach, which I shall call the legalistic, officials are expected to make a particular decision when facts are found that are specified under a normative standard (…) the propriety of the decision is evaluated in terms of fidelity to the applicable standard. This is not to imply that the legalistic approach is indifferent to consequences resulting from official action: those who fashion the standards are expected to make the necessary instrumental calculations and to design standards capable of advancing organizational goals." Damaška (1986), p. 21.

[21] "Hierarchical officialdom is subject to Parkinson's law and tends to expand its sphere of activity. Because it sharply separates internal from external spheres, it strives to monopolize procedural action (…) members of the private bar are denied a variety of functions in the legal process which, in proceedings before coordinate authority, are routinely performed by lawyers." Damaška (1986), p. 53.

[22] "Ideally, power is vested in amateurs who are called upon to perform authoritative functions *ad hoc*, or for a limited time. Where the apparatus of authority is in the hands of such temporary officials, there is little opportunity for a spirit of exclusivity to develop. Insiders and outsiders in relation to the judicial apparatus are not sharply distinguished, and the distinction is likely to be of little importance." Damaška (1986), p. 24.

[23] "The coordinate ideal rejects any approach to decision making that would require officials to apply standards divorced from prevailing ethical, political, or religious norms, or would compel them to reach results unsupported by common sense. In other words, 'technical' approaches to decision making appear undesirable." Damaška (1986), p. 27.

[24] "The ideal now under consideration envisages a wide distribution of authority among roughly equal lay officials: with no one clearly superior to others, there is essentially a single stratum of authority." Demonstrating how to maintain a sense of unity within a structure of this kind, the

logic of the state would also differ, reflecting a model in which the exercise of power involves greater dialogue with the population.[25]

Thus, by contrasting the two ideal types,[26] we can identify some central features: the first would be characterized essentially by the separation between professionals and laypersons, with a strong technical foundation. The second would be marked by a closer relationship between adjudicators and members of the community, exhibiting a lower degree of professionalism.

- In light of this, an important question arises: generally speaking, which side has the Western-style legal process tended to favor?

  We consider the answer to be quite clear. As seen at the beginning of this work, our civil procedure was shaped by a significant liberal influence, which led it to be incorporated into a power structure that closely resembles the hierarchical model described earlier.[27] Based on this, it was developed with a clear proposal for the centralization of power and an emphasis on technical criteria and specific texts. In a simplified depiction, these would be its most notable features.

It is certain that, in recent times, attempts to reassess this mode of operation in a more democratic sense have become commonplace, paving the way for new approaches.[28] This includes elements such as public hearings, increased involvement of the "third sector," and the establishment of ombudsman offices within the administrative sphere.[29] In all these cases, the aim is to confer legitimacy on state activity through dialogue[30], to establish a context more conducive to debate and participation.

---

author states that, due to the horizontal nature of the authority spectrum, "not unlike the situation in the international arena, the fear of reciprocity becomes a cohesive force, replacing the duty to submit to the imposed and the ordained that prevails in hierarchical organizations." Damaška (1986), p. 25.

[25] "Amateur officials draw no rigid lines between official and private domains. Accordingly, procedural steps can be taken informally in a private setting and can be interlaced with unofficial activity." Damaška (1986), p. 63.

[26] At this point, it is important to recall, with Max Weber, that ideal types "do not seek to schematically force the infinite and multifaceted historical life, but simply to create concepts useful for special purposes and orientation." In other words, the aim is not to reduce reality to a conceptual perspective, but merely to establish a mechanism that facilitates its understanding. See Weber (1982), p. 345.

[27] See Damaška (1986), pp. 29–38.

[28] In this regard, it is asserted that "democracy should be adopted as a procedure and as experimentation within communicative and argumentative action in order to reach the most morally correct decisions. However, it cannot usurp certain achievements, rights, and guarantees established by the Constitution (…) deliberation is legitimate if the inclusion of parties in the discussion and decision-making process occurs on an equal footing and without coercive pressures; with knowledge of the factual terms of the issue, and in such a way that minorities are not prevented from participating, at times when individuals are not subject to extreme emotions." Godoy (2012), pp. 108–109.

[29] On these topics, see Salamon and Anheier (1997), Falcão (2004), Lyra (2011), Gomes (2004).

[30] As stated by Gustavo Binenbojm, "the crises of representative democracy and formal law, the increasing allocation of decision-making responsibilities to the Public Administration through open-ended legal norms, as well as the proliferation of independent administrative authorities not

Furthermore, it is worth noting that the advocacy for this restoration has also become common in the field of procedural law.[31] Through concepts such as cooperation or collaboration, the aim is to bring the parties to the conflict (the judge and the litigants) closer together in a more horizontal and polycentric manner.[32] This issue was already addressed in the work of Calamandrei,[33] and has gained particular significance in recent years.

However, despite the growing prominence of this discourse, there remains a foundational pillar of the discipline that persists unchanged and appears to prevent its interpretation as a participatory field: its essentially technical and professionalized nature. In such a context, invoking democracy is questionable. Furthermore, it is not an exaggeration to state that dispute resolution currently takes place on a stage that is inaccessible and incomprehensible. It takes place in a setting that is, by its very nature, antidemocratic.

This issue is closely related to the civil procedure's attachment to rituals and concepts, as previously discussed in this chapter. As a result, the discipline develops

---

directly *responsive* to the political will of elected officials, are currently driving the almost universal—though not uncontroversial—trend of promoting social participation in the processes of formulating administrative decisions. Such is its importance today that it has already been considered a way to *democratize* representative democracies." Binenbojm (2006), p. 87.

[31] It is important to note, however, that this assessment of adequacy (based on ideal models) cannot be adopted simplistically. This caveat is raised by Fredie Didier Jr., who states that "doctrine often associates the adversarial-dispositive model with non-authoritarian, politically more liberal regimes, and the inquisitorial model with authoritarian, interventionist regimes (...) this inference is somewhat simplistic. While it is true that cultural factors will certainly influence the structure of the proceedings and the method of exercising power, there is no direct relationship between the increase of judicial powers and autocratic regimes, or the enhancement of the parties' role and democratic regimes. Neither is the dispositive process synonymous with a democratic process, nor does the inquisitorial process necessarily mean an authoritarian process." Didier Jr. (2010), p.76.

[32] See Nunes (2008).

[33] "The parties are *persons,* that is, subjects endowed with rights and duties, and they do not stand powerless before the judge, required to obey passively, but as free citizens who appear before him not only with obligations to fulfill, but also with rights to protect. And the judge is not only vested with authority over them but is a public servant, bound to them by duties and responsibilities, so that the parties have the right to express their opinions freely and to be heard attentively (...) therefore, the judge is never the sole actor in the judicial process. This process is not a monologue; it is a dialogue, a conversation, an exchange of proposals and responses, an interplay of actions and reactions, of attacks and counterattacks, of arguments and refutations." Calamandrei (1956), pp. 73–74.

its own capital.[34] It creates a divide between the technical and the layperson, a gap that unreflective daily practice tends only to widen.[35]

- After all, what are the meanings of terms such as *"data venia"* or *"a quo"*? What does "preclusion" represent, and what is its impact on the right asserted in court? How and when is it possible to seek the modification of a particular judicial decision? Why are some appeals filed directly with the Court while others are not?

The answer to this type of question is certainly not found in the vocabulary of those who have not undergone the specific training provided by law schools. As a result, civil procedure becomes enigmatic for the "ordinary" individual, taking on a dimension that is alien to their capacity for participation. This aspect is further reinforced and perpetuated by the common requirement that legal representation in court must be carried out by attorneys. From any perspective, there are numerous elements of exclusion imposed on the subject.

4.3 Civil Procedure as a Framework of Institutional Choices

As the final point to be examined in this chapter, we present another argument that engages with the previous considerations. In summary, by acknowledging that civil procedure is flexible and contextually determined, we must recognize that its development occurs through a series of successive choices. Its path allows for different routes, far removed from any purely linear design.

This aspect can be more clearly understood by considering an initial question: Is there, at the local or global level, a correct civil procedure?

---

[34] As incisively noted by Bourdieu, "the establishment of a entails the imposition of a boundary between those who are prepared to enter the game and those who, once thrown into it, in fact remain excluded, as they are unable to effect the conversion of their entire mental space—and, in particular, of their entire linguistic posture—required for entry into this social space. The constitution of a specifically legal competence, the technical mastery of a scientific knowledge often antithetical to the simple recommendations of common sense, leads to the disqualification of the layperson's sense of equity and the revocation of their spontaneous construction of the facts, their the case>. The gap between the ordinary perspective of the person who is to become a *litigant*, that is, a client, and the scientific perspective of the expert, judge, lawyer, legal advisor, etc., is not accidental; it is constitutive of a power relationship that underpins two different systems of assumptions, of expressive intentions—in short, two worldviews." Bourdieu (1989), pp. 225–226.

[35] According to Hespanha, "although it cannot be said that law is neutral with respect to interests or objectives related to power (…) the truth is that law appears as a relatively autonomous sphere, resistant to the influence of other spheres of social activity. This is often emphasized, both when referring to the way jurists resist adopting concepts foreign to their own way of thinking and speaking, and when highlighting how they cultivate a corporate spirit (…). Some elements of this alleged strategy of *distancing* from the world can be listed. One of them is the formalized character of legal language which, by making it difficult for outsiders to access, creates for jurists a monopoly on decisive knowledge about everyday life." Hespanha (2012), pp. 306–307.

As can be seen, the issue can unfold on two different levels. On the first level, related to a modern philosophical discourse,[36] the very existence of a procedural model capable of asserting itself universally is called into question. On the second, with a more modest scope, the focus is contingently limited, subject to territorial or cultural parameters. In this way, its dimension is substantially altered.

Starting at the first level, we identify that your project is extremely broad. In summary, it concerns the possibility of asserting that a particular form of dispute resolution is the *most appropriate* in hypothetical and absolute terms. In our view, this claim should be promptly dismissed. Given that we have repeatedly discussed the conjectural nature of the judicial process and its capacity for adaptation, any different response here would be devoid of meaning.

In this regard, it is also noteworthy that the attempt at intercultural transposition of dispute resolution models would be subject to the same criticisms that, about four decades ago, were leveled by Trubek and Galanter against legal knowledge itself in general[37], impacting the *law and development* argument and the defense of the strict importation of structures.[38] In short, it has become common to argue that the law cannot act in a vertical and imperative manner, imposing broad changes without being attentive to contextual aspects and specificities.[39]

---

[36] Elaborating on this point, Rouanet emphasizes that "the civilizational project of modernity is primarily composed of the concepts of universality, individuality, and autonomy. Universality means that it is intended for all human beings, regardless of national, ethnic, or cultural barriers. Individuality means that these human beings are regarded as concrete persons and not merely as members of a collective, and that their increasing individualization is ascribed positive ethical value. Autonomy means that these individualized human beings are capable of thinking for themselves, without the tutelage of religion or ideology, of acting in the public sphere, and of acquiring through their own labor the goods and services necessary for material survival." Subsequently, however, the author himself asserts that "this civilizational project is coming apart at the seams." See Rouanet (1993), p. 09.

[37] Thus, Trubek and Galanter (1974).

[38] Explaining this mentality, Davis and Trebilcock state that, "based on modernization theory, the first wave of law and development scholars that emerged in the 1960s assumed that the diffusion of Western law to the Third World would assist in its modernization. In effect, it was believed that modern law was the 'functional prerequisite of an industrial economy.' Influenced by Weber, a strong instrumentalist conception of law underpinned this view of the relationship between law and development. As defined by Burg, this conception 'regards law as a force that can be shaped and manipulated to alter human behavior and achieve development.' It 'focuses primarily on the substantive norms of law, expects the state to enact these norms, and reserves for the legal profession a prominent role in their formulation.' This conception of law as an instrument of development, and not merely as a response to it, as well as the view of the jurist as a 'social engineer,' was entirely consistent with the 'perceived need for directed and rapid change' that underlay the modernization school's notion of development." Subsequently, the same scholars demonstrate the diversity of forms assumed by *law and development* after the monopoly of this modernizing discourse was overcome. See, therefore, Davis and Trebilcock (2009), pp. 217–268. Likewise, Trubek and Santos (2006).

[39] Demonstrating the impact of this reasoning in the context of the relationship between law and development, see Davis and Trebilcock (2009).

In this regard, it is worth recalling once again the example previously mentioned, related to the dispute resolution model used by the Azande tribe in Africa. As demonstrated by Chase, the English attempt to replace this system with a structure more closely aligned with Western logic has, to this day, met with little acceptance.[40] Once again, we observe that the issue is one of legitimacy. There is no way to establish an *a priori* parameter, detached from the real world, that can universally address this matter.

Thus, the first possibility of referring to an *ideal* model of procedure does not seem appropriate to us. Given the cultural nature of the discipline, it is not possible to establish a structure that is supposedly superior to others, disregarding the audience and the setting of the performance. This leaves, therefore, the second line of inquiry, based on a more restricted and limited logic. For example, is it possible today to speak of a correct procedure for a given country?

- We consider the answer to this elementary question essential for a critical analysis of the procedural system. This is because, given its argumentative and flexible nature, we believe that the discipline will always be subject to the value judgments of its scholars. Its structure is in constant development, yet open to differing opinions regarding its next steps: while one architect may propose that a new floor be enclosed in glass, another professional may advocate for the use of tile cladding. Neither would be wrong. There would simply be a divergence of perspective.

Thus, we believe that even in a more limited environment, there is a clear difficulty in attempting to sustain the existence of a proper civil procedure. This is a legacy of the inherently rhetorical nature and the flexible character of the subject matter, which prevents any single argument from prevailing absolutely and excluding all others. The true/false dichotomy proves insufficient in this context, subjecting the development of the discipline to ongoing scrutiny through debate and persuasion.

Therefore, since we consider that the procedural system is opposed to definitive answers, we believe that its scholars must adopt a constant attitude of intellectual humility. Recognizing that the discipline can accommodate different perspectives, it is incumbent upon the scholar to justify why their approach is the most compatible with a given context. However, this does not render their position an unassailable truth, nor does it preclude debate within the realms of legal doctrine, legislation, and the courts. Civil procedural law is shaped by choices, and it is within these domains that such choices are made.

---

40 "Under British rule, which began around the turn of the nineteenth century, oracular justice was censored and the Zande kings lost most of their authority over legal disputes. The Azande were not receptive to the new system of dispute resolution imposed by the British, since the judgment of oracles was no longer accepted: '[T]hey do not approve of European methods, because in their view the only concrete proof of guilt or innocence is not permitted.' Even the accused preferred the traditional method of fact-finding, because under European procedures they could be convicted based solely on the testimony of a woman." Chase (2014), pp. 52–53.

Moreover, by acknowledging that to conceptualize the judicial process is to make choices among different paths, we also believe that its course inevitably involves sacrifices and concessions. Only in this way can one prevent the subject matter from coexisting with a prodigal discourse or with mutually inconsistent arguments. In such cases, an undesirable seesaw is created: by attempting to push it in opposite directions, success is achieved in neither.

- In our view, this issue can be symbolized by the ongoing attempt to fully reconcile, within a single procedural framework, the values of participation and efficiency. Although both are important, their alignment appears to create an inevitable bottleneck. After all, is it possible to accommodate both aspects without any form of *compromise*?

We believe not. Although the theorist may legitimately choose to prioritize either side, we maintain that it is impossible to reconcile them without accepting that one will inevitably be compromised to a greater extent. Between means and ends, there is no choice that can encompass everything. Advocating for "full adversarial proceedings" necessarily reduces efficiency, and vice versa.[41] Every option entails a cost, and it is up to the scholar to acknowledge and assume responsibility for these consequences.

This thus constitutes yet another vector for the analysis of civil procedure. On the one hand, it is necessary to understand that its construction requires making choices. On the other hand, we must note that these choices will involve dilemmas and sacrifices, demanding a constant foundation of coherence. In summary, it is not possible to seriously promise everything. Any hypothesis related to civil procedural law must be confronted with this reality.

References

Alexy, R. (1993). *Teoria de los derechos fundamentales*. Centro de Estudios Constitucionales.
Amaral, G. (2001). *Direito, escassez e escolha*. Renovar.
Binenbojm, G. (2006). *A constitucionalização do Direito Administrativo: um itinerário de avanços e retrocessos. Revista Brasileira de Direito Público*, 14.
Bourdieu, P. (1989). *O Poder Simbólico*. Lisboa.
Calabresi, G., & Bobbit, P. (1978). *Tragic choices*. W.W. Norton & Company.
Calamandrei, P. (1956). *Procedure and democracy*. New York University Press.

[41] As already recognized by Ovídio Baptista da Silva, "either the proceedings penalize the claimant, burdening them with all the costs arising from the time required to reach a final resolution of the *dispute*, in order to ensure that the outcome of the proceedings corresponds, as much as possible, to a judgment of justice and certainty; or, conversely, if the legislator accepts the premise that not all claims and social demands possess the same political significance or require the same urgency of immediate realization, certain claims are distinguished and granted a privileged status within the proceedings, so that between the two inherent poles of the legal phenomenon—namely, the demand for justice and security, on the one hand, and the *effectiveness* of the rights proclaimed by the legislator, on the other—the choice is made for the latter expectation to be achieved at the expense, now no longer of the claimant (…), but rather of the defendant." Silva (1993), p. 155.

Cavallone, B. (2010). In difesa dela Veriphobia (considerazioni amichevolmente polemiche su un libro recente di Michele Taruffo. *Rivista di Diritto Processuale*, 65.

Chase, O. G. (2014). *Direito, Cultura e Ritual*. Editora Marcial Pons.

Clève, C. M. (2006). A Eficácia dos Direitos Fundamentais Sociais. *Revista de Direito Constitucional e Internacional, 54*.

Damaška, M. (1986). *The faces of justice and state authority*. Yale University Press.

Davis, K. E., & Trebilcock, M. J. (2009). A relação entre direito e desenvolvimento: otimistas versus céticos. *Revista Direito GV*. 5.

Didier, F., Jr. (2010). *Curso de Direito Processual Civil* (Vol. 1, 12th ed.). Editora JusPodivm.

Falcão, J. (2004). *Democracia, Direito e Terceiro Setor*. Editora FGV.

Frank, J. (1949). *Courts on trial*. Princeton University Press.

Galdino, F. (2005). *Introdução à Teoria dos Custos dos Direitos – Direitos não nascem em árvores*. Editora Lumen Juris.

Godoy, M. G. (2012). *Constitucionalismo e Democracia – Uma leitura a partir de Carlos Santiago Nino e Roberto Gargarella*. São Paulo.

Gomes, M. E. A. C. (2004). Do Instituto do Ombudsman à construção das ouvidorias públicas no Brasil. In R. P. Lyra (Ed.), *Autônomas x obedientes: a ouvidoria pública em debate*. João Pessoa.

Haack, S. (1996). Concern for truth: What it means, why it matters. In P. R. Gross, N. Levitt, & M. W. Lewis (Eds.), *The flight from science and reason*. New York Academy of Science.

Hespanha, A. M. (2012). *O Caleidoscópio do Direito*. Lisboa.

Holmes, S., & Sunstein, C. R. (2000). *The cost of rights – why liberty depends on taxes*. W.W Norton & Company.

Jones, B. D. (1999). Bounded rationality. *Annual Review of Political Science, 2*.

Kornhausen, L. (2012). Judicial organization and administration. In C. W. Sanchirico (Ed.), *Procedural law and economics*. Edward Elgar.

Lyra, R. P. (2011). *Do Tribuno da Plebe ao Ouvidor Público: estudos sobre defensores da cidadania*. Editora UFPB.

Mancuso, R. C. (2014). *A resolução dos conflitos e a função judicial no contemporâneo Estado de Direito* (2nd ed.). Ed. RT.

Nunes, D. J. C. (2008). *Processo jurisdicional democrático: uma análise crítica das reformas processuais*. Juruá.

Posner, R. (2008). *How judges think*. Harvard University Press.

Ragone, A. P. (2016). La revalorización de la audiencia preliminar o preparatoria: una mirada desde la justicia distributiva en el proceso civil. *Revista de Processo., 252*.

Rorty, R. (1993). *Contingency, irony and solidarity*. Cambridge University Press.

Rouanet, S. P. (1993). *Mal-estar na modernidade*. Companhia das Letras.

Salamon, L. M., & Anheier, H. K. (1997). *Defining the nonprofit sector: A crossnational analysis*. Manchester University Press.

Sarlet, I. W. (2009). *A eficácia dos direitos fundamentais – uma teoria geral dos direitos fundamentais na perspectiva constitucional* (10th ed.). Livraria do Advogado.

Schauer, F. (2009). *Thinking like a lawyer – A new introduction to legal reasoning*. Harvard University Press.

Silva, O. A. B. (1993). A "Plenitude de Defesa" no Processo Civil. In S. F. Teixeira (Ed.), *As Garantias do Cidadão na Justiça*. Saraiva.

Sundfeld, C. A. (2009). *Fundamentos do Direito Público*. Malheiros.

Taruffo, M. (2010). Contro la veriphobia. Osservazioni sparse in risposta a Bruno Cavallone. *Rivista di Diritto Processuale*, 65.

Torrano, B. (2014). *Do fato à legalidade: introdução à teoria analítica do direito*. Lumen Juris.

Trubek, D., & Galanter, M. (1974). Scholars in self-estrangement: Some reflections on the crisis in law and development studies in the United States. *Wisconsin Law Review, 4*.

Trubek, D., & Santos, A. (2006). *The new law and economical development – A critical appraise*. Cambridge University Press.

Weber, M. (1982). *Ensaios de sociologia*. LTC Editora.

Chapter 5
Critically Reconstructing Civil Procedure

5.1 Bringing Elements Together: Proportionality and Civil Procedure

The considerations presented thus far demonstrate that understanding the judicial process critically means recognizing new dimensions within its reality: by identifying its cultural and adaptable nature, we realize that the discipline is constantly subject to doubts and inquiries. By seeking to bring its theory closer to its concrete possibilities, we observe the existence of various boundaries imposed by the real world. In summary, the argument reveals a scenario characterized by the complexity of both limitations and possibilities.

In light of this scenario, we believe there is a central guiding principle to be explored in order to achieve the optimal structuring of the discipline: proportionality, in its broadest sense. In our view, it is from this benchmark that a more coherent discourse can be constructed, articulating in a sound and comprehensive manner the various factors that permeate procedural practice.

To some extent, the notion of proportionality is not new to legal proceedings. On the contrary, it is an issue embedded in its everyday lexicon, regularly serving as a guiding principle for its practitioners. Thus, when applying a particular rule, it is common for the judge to assess whether its application is proportionate. Similarly, when determining whether a specific right should be granted in a given case, it is routine for the assessment of its proportionality to serve as an essential filter.

In all these cases, the operation of the proceedings places the parameter as a key element. It is true that this does not always occur in a technical manner, as noted by Virgílio Afonso da Silva.[1] In any event, what is most important here is to recognize

[1] In the author's words, "when, in legal discourse, one refers to the principle of reasonableness or to the principle or rule of proportionality, it is evident that these terms carry a technical-legal connotation and are no longer synonymous, as they express distinct legal constructs. It may be admit-

G. Osna, *Civil Procedure, Culture, and Proportionality*,
https://doi.org/10.1007/978-3-032-27555-4_5

that, in such instances, the recourse to proportionality is usually situated within the realm of substantive law. It is a criterion that (with greater or lesser specificity) conditions the solution to be given to the case, rather than the proceedings themselves.

- To illustrate the point, let us consider a situation in which it is now common for our Courts to resort to the argument in question. For this purpose, imagine that "X," a well-known politician, becomes aware that the weekly newspaper "Y" is about to publish a story concerning his personal life that infringes upon his honor. Let us further suppose that "X" seeks to prevent the publication of the article and therefore files an injunction with the court for this purpose.

In this situation, an unavoidable conflict between principles would arise: on one hand, freedom of the press; on the other, the right to privacy.[2] In this type of dispute, it is quite likely that, at some point, recourse would be made to proportionality in some dimension: would the restriction on the possibility of communication be proportional? Would it be necessary and appropriate for such a limitation to be imposed?

Questions such as these are commonplace in our forensic practice, making the use of this criterion quite frequent as well. In any case, in this type of scenario, the application of the standard would end up affecting only the material provision itself, affecting the interference to be introduced into the concrete world and its network of positions. Thus, it would not be questioned whether the procedure established for this purpose would be proportionate or whether the means employed would possess this attribute. And this level of scrutiny seems to us to be essential.

But how would this type of analysis affect civil procedural law? In what forms and at what moments would it affect it? What kind of developments would this interpretative possibility bring to the field?

---

ted that they have similar objectives, but this does not justify treating them as synonyms." In this sense, it should be emphasized that "the rule of proportionality in the review of laws restricting fundamental rights emerged from the jurisprudential development of the German Constitutional Court and is not merely a guideline that vaguely suggests that state actions should be reasonable, nor is it simply an analysis of the means-end relationship. As developed by German constitutional jurisprudence, it has a rationally defined structure, with independent sub-elements—the analysis of suitability, necessity, and proportionality in the strict sense—which are applied in a predefined order and confer upon the rule of proportionality the individuality that clearly distinguishes it from the mere requirement of reasonableness." Silva (2002), p. 23.

[2] As previously stated, "while we recognize the existence of a close relationship between freedom of the press and democracy, particular attention must be given to the potential conflict between the exercise of this freedom and the protection of individual fundamental rights, which may result in a clash with the very safeguarding of human dignity. Understanding this scenario reveals that at the core of the debate lies a dangerous minefield, presenting a clear challenge to legal interpretation. Indeed, although it serves as an important lever for the formation and consolidation of democratic foundations, the press's power to inform is in constant tension with the sphere of protection afforded to individual rights. This conflict becomes evident when the dissemination of news may cause clear harm to the person reported on and violate their dignity (…) in such cases, on one side stands the protection of freedom of the press, whose significance has already been demonstrated, and on the other, the defense of the individual, (…) established by the 1988 Federal Constitution as a foundation of our Republic." On this topic, see Osna (2012), pp. 17–41.

In addressing these questions, it is clear that, at first glance, the principle of proportionality could be related to the subject matter from an endoprocedural perspective. Simply put, there would be a constant risk that different values inherent to the proceedings might come into conflict, thus requiring an assessment of accommodation tailored to the demands of the case.

As noted by Arenhart, this preliminary interpretation arises from the very axiological plurality that characterizes the resolution of disputes, potentially generating different challenges from specific debates.[3] In any given proceeding, there is a constant possibility that urgency will come into conflict with legal certainty or that participation will clash with effectiveness. Amidst this tangle of factors, it is the role of the proceedings to seek the most proportionate response.

However, alongside this issue, we believe that the criterion of proportionality should also come into play in dispute resolution from another perspective. This refers to what Arenhart calls pan-procedural proportionality. Through this second lens, whether in shaping the foundations of the discipline or in its application in daily legal practice, it is necessary to consider the broader circumstances that surround it. The scope of observation is expanded, requiring a greater number of aspects to be brought to the forefront.[4]

- In general terms, the core of this idea lies in a specific point: civil procedure can never be conceived based on an isolated conflict. Whether in judicial activity or legislative action, it is necessary to consider the institutional capacity of the Judiciary, also examining the cultural and political elements that permeate the jurisdiction. Issues arise, such as the need to ensure that the time allocated to each case does not compromise the consideration of others, thereby readjusting the procedural framework according to a criterion of proportionality that goes

[3] Explaining this initial approach, Arenhart notes that, within the scope of constitutional principles, "in most situations such guarantees come into conflict and must be harmonized, under penalty of one fundamental precept prevailing over the others. To avoid such superposition and with the aim of reconciling the principles, both doctrine and case law, drawing from the German experience, employ the criterion of proportionality. According to this precept, the balancing of various conflicting constitutional principles—in order to reach the best solution for the specific case—must be guided by three sub-criteria: the act must be assessed (…) in terms of its suitability, necessity, and proportionality (…) this analysis of proportionality, here referred to as endoprocedural proportionality, is commonly used to assess the reconciliation, for example, between the principles of timeliness of relief (…) and the adversarial process." Arenhart (2013), pp. 34–35.

[4] "In this other dimension of proportionality, the process itself is not examined in isolation. Rather, the judicial activity is assessed in terms of the relationship between the state effort devoted to a specific case and the entirety of judicial proceedings (existing or potential) that are equally entitled to the same effort. In this regard, given the scarcity of state resources, the degree of effectiveness granted to a single proceeding must be considered in light of the need to ensure the efficiency of the judicial system as a whole (…) from this perspective, the criteria of necessity, suitability, and proportionality (…) acquire new contours. Indeed, the inquiry into the reasonableness of the procedural treatment given to an individual case is no longer examined solely within its own context (…) the solution, in summary (…) operates on another level: the macroscopic one." Arenhart (2013), pp. 38–39.

beyond the mere analysis of the individual case.[5] It is on this basis that its institutions could achieve a better balance.

After all, is it appropriate for the judge not to have integrated control over the disputes under their jurisdiction? Is it feasible for them to devote equal attention to all cases? Can one consider a normative reform of the procedure without addressing its material capacity?

It is in response to this type of argument that the pan-procedural discourse takes shape. Indeed, the procedural system ceases to be merely a forum for debating the proportionality of factual intervention and must itself also be proportionate to its actual possibilities.[6]

From this perspective, the concept of proportionality could facilitate the connection between the theoretical judicial process and the judicial process as it occurs in reality, allowing for the articulation of structural, cultural, and legislative factors related to the subject matter.[7] As described in the previous section, the application of this new criterion would enable a decisive dialogue with the global possibilities

[5] Presenting the issue, it was emphasized that "this base of analysis and the associated macro perspective are clearly in harmony with the requirements of the complexity of contemporary civil litigation. In this context, the pan-procedural approach contributes to the modulation of adjudication in a way that considers the judiciary as a whole, highlighting its barriers and providing an isonomic distribution of procedural activity among all cases awaiting resolution. The design suggests that, once this approach is adopted, each case ceases to be seen as an isolated piece, and the puzzle is understood from a global perspective. A natural consequence of this is that, considering the limits of the public budget, the efforts devoted to a case should be harmonized with the institutional effectiveness of the judiciary. Each case should be treated equally, establishing a new requirement based on parameters of necessity, adequacy, and proportionality. Thus, every response and every collision of fundamental rights begins to be viewed on another level: the macroscopic level." Arenhart and Osna (2014), p. 199.

[6] "Thus understood, the principle of proportionality can be situated within the Italian procedural experience as an aspect of the constitutional value of efficiency in the regulation of procedure, which is inferred from the assertion of reasonable duration (…) in this context, assessments emerge that are, by definition, distinct from one legal system to another, and also vary within the same legal system over time, since they require consideration of the state of justice administration resources in a given system at a particular historical moment." Caponi (2011), p. 405.

[7] "Adjudication is an activity that must necessarily be provided by the State to anyone who feels that the exercise of their rights has been threatened or violated. However, this service may, in turn, be deficient in three specific dimensions: (a) legislative, (b) structural, and (c) cultural (…) The analysis of each of these elements is usually conducted separately, assigning each to a distinct field of legal studies (such as anthropology or sociology). Nevertheless, we argue that their interconnection is profound enough to require their collective consideration when discussing adjudication or civil procedure and its reforms (…) Consequently, examining the relationship among these three elements requires the selection of a parameter capable of harmonizing them and facilitating their dialogue and application. This is because the adequacy of adjudication can only be assessed when all three dimensions are taken into account. It is precisely here that we believe proportionality, in its pan-procedural approach, can be situated, serving as a filter that enables permeability among the three dimensions, providing the necessary foundation for a use of civil procedure that is compatible with its global premises and consequences." Arenhart and Osna (2014), pp. 197–199.

and needs related to procedural practice, impacting both its legislative structure and its specific application.

- The issue can be further illustrated by another example. Let us suppose that two proceedings involving the banking institution "X" are pending before the same court. In one case, consumer "H" seeks compensation for various fees that were charged to him monthly, amounting to a small sum. In the other, "X" is the defendant in a class action brought by a consumer protection association, challenging practices repeatedly adopted against all its account holders and seeking compensation in the millions.

In this context, it is clear that the financial institution would not devote equal attention to both claims. Likewise, there is no doubt that the social impact brought about by each would not be uniform either.[8] Given this, should the Judiciary assign the same weight to each case? Would it be mistaken to assert that, due to their differing characteristics, these measures should also be treated differently? How can procedural action be adapted to such discrepancies, considering the scarcity of resources and the system's actual capacity for response?

In identifying the issues, we realize that the adoption of pan-procedural logic would certainly facilitate the answers. With this approach, allocating different resources to each dispute (according to its specificities) would not only be feasible but also advisable. Instead of formal equality, the focus would shift to sufficiency—requiring a constant comparison between the circumstances of the dispute and its real possibilities.[9]

Finally, to carry out this type of analysis, we consider that the discourse of orthodox civil procedure will not always be sufficient, suggesting the need for its ongoing

---

[8] Indeed, it is important here to recall the distinction between the *private* value of a given lawsuit (that is, the value perceived by the parties themselves when assessing their own circumstances) and its *public* value (that is, the social impact resulting from its capacity to influence behavior). Elaborating on this issue, Miceli notes that "Shavell (…) was the first to explicitly compare the private and the social value of lawsuits in a costly legal system. He pointed out that, while the private value of a suit depends solely on a plaintiff's comparison of the payment he or she expects to receive at trial with the cost of filing suit, the social value depends on the extent to which lawsuits induce the defendant to undertake socially desirable accident prevention. A key finding was that there is no necessary connection between these two values. That is, a suit may be privately valuable but not socially valuable, or the reverse may be true. As a result, in an unrestricted legal system, there may be either too much or too little litigation from a social perspective." Miceli (2012). Shavell (1982), pp. 333–339.

[9] It is worth noting here that theorists such as Frankfurter attribute a broader meaning to this shift, arguing that this is the logic that should govern the very analysis of social justice; that concern with equality would be ineffective, as there is no moral value to be protected in this regard; and that it is preferable to place the sufficiency of resources as the central parameter. In summary, a community with internal differences would not be problematic if everyone had enough; conversely, an environment of absolute equality could be useless and undesirable if everyone's situation were precarious. Thus, Frankfurter (2015).

dialogue with fields such as Economics and Management.[10] In this way, it becomes possible to more clearly analyze aspects such as its management[11] and its influence on social behaviors,[12] in a broad and proportional manner. The path is challenging, but the complexity of the issues at hand seems to make it highly recommended.

[10] Observing the importance of this topic, Kornhausen points out that "economic analyses of substantive legal rules generally suppress the adjudication of factual and legal disputes that a legal rule might engender. The nature of adjudication, however, will influence greatly both the content of the substantive law and the costs of dispute resolution. An understanding of the structure of adjudication is thus central to an understanding of the effects of legal rules on behavior and on the identification of socially desirable legal rules. In addition, adjudication is a complex task implemented through institutions that vary across time and jurisdiction. The structure of adjudication and questions of judicial organization and administration thus present a rich field of study in their own right." Kornhausen (2012), p. 308.

[11] On this subject, it should be noted that "efforts to reform management models within organizations of the Judiciary, while seeking references in these new ideas, will naturally be focused on the specific characteristics of the sector. It bears repeating, whenever appropriate, that a point of vital importance to guide any management reform initiatives in the Judiciary is its effective independence. Furthermore, what values are intended to be protected? What values are intended to be changed? An environment of judicial stability and security constitutes a critical requirement for efforts aimed at the country's economic and social development, whether regarding actions undertaken by the private sector or the capacity to govern (…) Rethinking management structures and processes for the Judiciary, in line with the broader movement of public sector reform, entails identifying and adapting new concepts, ideas, and practices to the nature and peculiarities of the role of justice in social relations." Cunha (2010), p. 146.

[12] In the words of Cooter and Ulen, "we can say that economics provides a behavioral theory to predict how people respond to changes in law. This theory surpasses intuition, just as science surpasses common sense. In addition to a scientific theory of behavior, economics provides a useful normative standard for evaluating law and policy. Laws are not just arcane technical arguments; they are instruments for achieving important social goals. In order to know the effects of laws on those goals, judges and other lawmakers must have a method of evaluating laws' effects on important social values. Economics predicts the effects of policies on efficiency (…) besides efficiency, economics predicts the effects of policies on another important value: *distribution*." In the same vein, examining the issue within Brazilian academia, Luciano Timm notes: "Why should Law engage in dialogue with and draw closer to Economics? Briefly, first, because Economics is the science that adequately describes the behavior of human beings interacting in the market, which is so important for real life in society. Second, because economics is a behavioral science that has achieved a respectable and considerable scientific standard, and is today one of the leading fields among the applied social sciences due to the degree of mathematical and econometric validation of its models. Third, Economic Science is concerned with the efficient management of scarce social resources to meet unlimited human needs—which is a key issue when discussing social rights or, more generally, fundamental rights." Cooter and Ulen (2000), pp. 03–04. Timm (2008), p. 54.

5.2 Proportionality and Civil Procedure in Comparative Perspective

Furthermore, when we put into perspective the main aspects of this broad proportionality assessment, we recognize that its use is not unprecedented in the procedural field.[13] Sharing some of the premises and concerns discussed throughout this work, different jurisdictions have already explicitly established this type of guideline as a criterion for procedural conduct. This is not a mere mental inference, but an argument with significant concrete support.

Indeed, a primary (and most obvious) example of legislative construction grounded in the approach proposed here is found in the English *Civil Procedure Rules*. There, the central function of the proceedings is to ensure that the case is adjudicated justly, emphasizing that "*dealing with a case justly includes, so far as is practicable: (a) ensuring that the parties are on an equal footing; (b) saving expense; (c) dealing with the case in ways which are proportionate: (i) to the amount of money involved; (ii) to the importance of the case; (iii) to the complexity of the issues; and (iv) to the financial position of each party; (d) ensuring that it is dealt with expeditiously and fairly; and (e) allotting to it an appropriate share of the court's resources, while taking into account the need to allot resources to other cases.*"[14]

Thus, as noted by Ragone,[15] the text adopts as its guiding principle the need for the proceedings to maintain constant vigilance regarding their material feasibility, setting aside purely theoretical constructs. From this perspective, the idea of proportionality, as suggested here, is placed in a central, leading role.[16]

---

[13] Describing the issue in greater detail, it was stated on another occasion that "we believe that proportionality can also be used as a tool of *judicial* management. From this perspective, such a principle could be seen as an interpretative element capable of contributing to the resolution of the puzzles of contemporary civil litigation observed in the previous section. In the challenge posed by its functions and its material constraints, we believe that this approach can contribute both on an '*endo-procedural*' side (as more commonly noted) and, especially, in what we call the '*pan-procedural*' one." Arenhart and Osna (2014), p. 196.

[14] This is the original text of The Civil Procedure Rules 1998, Part 1.

[15] "If we analyze the first rule of the English Civil Procedure Rules, we can identify a teleological postulate and instrumental references, that is, what these rules are for and how to achieve the stated objectives. The first is to provide a fair and proportionate treatment of cases in relation to their cost (ends). The second implies that, for the treatment of cases according to criteria of justice and proportionality, the following must be considered: the equality of the parties in the proceedings, the cost (financial, temporal) and the parties' ability to bear it, the importance and complexity of the issues involved, and the proportionate allocation of resources and efforts to the case (means). This allocation of resources is not only focused on a current case to be heard by a court, but should also take into account that there are and will be other cases that will require the judiciary's infrastructure and human resources." Ragone (2016).

[16] "Proportionality is a truly novel aspect as a guiding principle of civil justice. It is no longer accepted that a correct decision must be reached at any cost, even at the expense of the rights of the party seeking protection (which may be granted late or insufficiently). Proportionality does not require precision and applies to at least two dimensions: (i) to the parties, insofar as the revaluation

Delving deeper into this issue, it is also relevant to highlight that the reasons and purposes underlying the legislative framework are closely connected to various aspects discussed in the preceding pages. In summary, the reforms that led to the current English model, conceived by Lord Woolf, explicitly pursued three essential objectives: (1) to improve access to justice and reduce the inherent costs of litigation; (2) to reduce the complexity of the rules and modernize the terminology associated with the proceedings; and (3) finally, to eliminate unnecessary distinctions between procedural reality and the procedural framework.[17]

Based on this, some goals and objectives were established in alignment with a more critical perspective of the discipline. In this regard, seeking to address the costs, delays, and complexity of the proceedings,[18] the following postulates were set forth: (1) the system should be fair in its outcomes; (2) the system should be correct, ensuring the parties equal opportunities despite their differences; (3) the system should allow each litigant to challenge the allegations made against them; (4) the system should treat like cases equally.[19]

In addition to these guidelines, other recommendations were also established that align with the concerns advocated here: (1) procedures and their costs should be proportional to the nature of the issues involved; (2) cases should be resolved relatively quickly; (3) the judicial process should be understandable to its users and responsive to their needs; (4) the judicial process should provide the most reliable outcome possible, given the circumstances of the case; and (5) finally, the judicial

of the preliminary or preparatory hearing from the perspective of distributive justice in civil proceedings broadens the horizon of access to justice and allows for proceedings to be conducted at appropriate costs and within a reasonable timeframe; (ii) in relation to the court, which must consider a current case and the resources allocated to it, contextualizing it among other cases it will have to hear and decide in the future—'considering the amount of resources spent on each case in light of the need to ensure that appropriate judicial resources are available for other litigants.'" Ragone (2016).

[17] In the initial report on the reforms, the following was stated: "I was appointed by the Lord Chancellor on 28 March 1994 to review the current rules and procedures of the civil courts in England and Wales. The aims of the review were: to improve access to justice and reduce the cost of litigation; to reduce the complexity of the rules and modernise terminology; to remove unnecessary distinctions of practice and procedure."

[18] "The most recent report on the civil justice system as a whole was the Civil Justice Review, which was established in February 1985 with the following terms of reference: 'To improve the machinery of civil justice in England and Wales by means of reforms in jurisdiction, procedure and court administration and in particular to reduce delay, cost and complexity.'"

[19] "In considering the problems of the civil justice system I have kept in mind the basic principles that a civil justice system should fulfill to ensure access to justice: It should be just in the outcomes it delivers; It should be fair and be perceived as such by: ensuring that litigants have an equal opportunity, regardless of their resources, to assert or defend their legal rights; providing every litigant with an adequate opportunity to present their own case and respond to their opponent's; treating like cases alike."

process should be effective in the allocation of its resources and in its organization.[20]

- It was from this reorganization that, in order to allow for this adjustment between needs and possibilities, the decision-making structure was significantly altered: whereas previously a predominantly free logic prevailed, guided by the will of the parties, it became necessary to establish greater managerial control (*case management*) by the adjudicating body.[21] Moreover, the notion of proportionality became central to this arrangement.[22] The effectiveness of the proceedings should be aligned with their material possibilities, approaching procedural rules with greater skepticism and seeking to bring theory closer to the actual conditions of practice.[23]

---

[20] "Procedures and cost should be proportionate to the nature of the issues involved; it should address cases with reasonable speed; it should be understandable to those who use it; it should be responsive to the needs of its users; it should provide as much certainty as the nature of particular cases allows; it should be effective: adequately resourced and organized so as to give effect to the preceding principle."

[21] As highlighted by Zuckerman, "at the outset of his Interim Report Lord Woolf identified the cause of high costs as being not so much the complexity of procedure as the 'uncontrolled nature of the litigation process.' Without effective judicial control,' he says, '… the adversarial process is likely to encourage an adversarial culture and to degenerate into an environment in which the litigation process is too often seen as a battlefield where no rules apply.'" Based on this, the author noted that "Lord Woolf believes that in order to prevent litigious excesses we need to impose judicial control on litigation. The thrust of his strategy, therefore, is aimed at placing the litigation process under firm controls. These controls are to take two principal forms. The first is rule control (…) the second form of control would involve judicial supervision." Zuckerman (1996), p. 775.

[22] "The new CPR system recognized and sought to promote these principles, values, or aims: (1) proportionality, (2) procedural equality, (3) active judicial involvement in a case's progress, (4) accelerated access to justice through improved summary procedures, (5) curbing excessive documentary disclosure, (6) greater use of costs orders as a disciplinary measure, (7) limiting appeals, (8) encouraging settlement by using costs incentives to induce acceptance of reasonable settlement offers, and (9) judicial encouragement of recourse to ADR, notably mediation. These basic points are elaborated in the following paragraphs. 'The Overriding Objective' in CPR Part 1 gives prominence to the notion of 'proportionality' both in the organization of procedural levels—small claims, fast-track, or multi-track proceedings—and in the exercise of the court's extensive case management powers." Andrews (2012), pp. 04–05.

[23] "Case management has three main functions: to encourage the parties to pursue mediation, where this is practicable; secondly, to prevent the case from progressing too slowly and inefficiently; finally, to ensure that judicial resources are allocated proportionately, as required by 'the Overriding Objective' in CPR Part 1." Idem. p. 12. It is true that some reservations have been raised regarding this approach and its concrete results. In particular, Zuckerman's position concerning the path taken by the program deserves mention, as he argues that the suggested logic underestimated the *personal interest* of lawyers in the complexity of the proceedings. For them, the *more incomprehensible* and *protracted* the dispute resolution process, the higher the fees that could be earned—laying bare the agency relationship presented here. In the author's words, "Lord Woolf has sought to bring about a cultural change. He has proposed measures for reducing the cost and duration of litigation and for achieving a measure of reasonable proportionality between the value of the subject matter in dispute and the cost of the legal resolution. His primary aim is to reduce the amount of work involved in litigation and thereby costs. He proposes to achieve this by judicial

Alongside this provision in English law, it is also worth mentioning the recent adoption of this approach in United States civil procedure. There, the mindset has specifically impacted evidentiary matters, altering the structure of discovery and introducing a new element to its understanding.

Historically, the discovery phase has represented a significant expression of the American liberal mindset in the context of dispute resolution.[24] At this stage, the main aspects related to the scope and initiative of evidence production were established. While the role of the judge was conceived in a limited manner, broad latitude was granted to the parties. In general, the initiative was placed entirely in the hands of private individuals, advocating for minimal state intervention and reinforcing the very dialogue between civil procedure and its cultural background.

It was from this perspective that *Rule 26(b)(1)* assigned a "*broad and liberal*" scope to the issue.[25] According to its terms, the parties were permitted to request the production of evidence related to any and all facts hypothetically relevant to the dispute, whether connected to the initial claims or to the defense of any of the litigants.[26] This gave rise to an exhaustive evidentiary process, establishing a framework that persisted for decades.[27]

---

case management, which will pass the control over the intensity and pace of the litigious process from lawyers to judges. He also envisages greater standardization of procedure whereby straightforward cases will be litigated by fast simplified process. Admirable as these proposals are, they do not directly address the cause of high costs. The high level of costs is the natural outcome of the economic incentives possessed by lawyers, whose remuneration rises as litigation becomes more complicated and lengthy." Zuckerman (1996), p. 795.

[24] Explaining the issue, Bone noted that "discovery is the process by which parties obtain information from one another and from otherwise uncooperative third parties. The United States is unusual among the nations of the world for the extremely broad scope of discovery it allows (…) For example, the Federal Rules of Civil Procedure (FRCP) authorize discovery in federal court cases 'regarding any matter, not privileged, that is relevant to the claim or defense of any party' and state that 'relevant information need not be admissible at the trial if the discovery appears reasonably calculated to lead to the discovery of admissible evidence.' Bone (2012), p. 188.

[25] "The 'broad and liberal discovery' standard first appeared in the United States in 1938, when the Federal Rules of Civil Procedure were promulgated. With thirty-five states having adopted the federal rules as their own in the years since, the rule of 'broad and liberal' discovery established by current Rule 26(b)(1) now dominates in both federal and state courts. Under Rule 26(b)(1), parties are presumptively entitled to unearth any fact 'relevant' to the case—and to do so at the expense of the other party—unless the opposing party blocks the discovery. It is an invitation few litigants decline or avoid, if they dare to enter the courthouse. Broad discovery functioned without widespread dissatisfaction for decades after Rule 26 was enacted." Netzorg and Kern (2010), p. 514.

[26] "26(b)(1). Parties may obtain discovery regarding any matter, not privileged, which is relevant to the subject matter involved in the pending action, whether it relates to the claim or defense of the party seeking discovery or to the claim or defense of any other party."

[27] "The U.S. Supreme Court made clear from the onset of modern discovery that the scope of discovery authorized by Rule 26 was to be construed broadly and liberally. In its oft-quoted 1947 opinion in Hickman v. Taylor, the Court declared that the common cry of a 'fishing expedition' no longer would be sufficient to block discovery; instead, litigants must 'disgorge whatever facts' they may have that are 'relevant' to the subject matter." Netzorg and Kern (2010), p. 518.

Given the breadth of this structure, it is almost intuitive that its misuse could lead to excesses—unnecessarily hindering procedural activity. Such criticism has become common,[28] giving rise to several central dilemmas: does broad *discovery* possess intrinsic value, or is it subject to reform[29]? Do its potential benefits outweigh its possible disadvantages[30]?

Starting from this puzzle, it gradually came to be argued that the matter should be anchored by a judgment more closely aligned with concrete needs—specifically, by reasoning based on proportionality in the macro sense proposed here.

In practical terms, this interpretation had a decisive impact on the positive legal framework of the United States. Based on it, various legislative reforms were

---

[28] "There has been widespread criticism of the abuse of discovery." That statement comes not from a recent edition of the Defense Research Institute newsletter but from the Advisory Committee notes to the 1980 amendment that gave us the Rule 26(f) conference. Discovery abuse and the increase in the cost of litigation that flows from such abuse has been a constant theme emerging from analysis of the civil justice system (…) that theme continued to be explored by researchers during the mid-1990s. As one contemporary study of the American civil justice system observed, "[c]ases in federal courts take too long and cost litigants too much. Consequently, proponents of reform argue, some litigants are denied access to justice and many litigants incur inappropriate burdens when they turn to the courts for assistance in resolving disputes." Carroll (2010), p. 455.

[29] "So is discovery an expensive, burdensome thing whose abuses must be curbed, and coercive power minimized, whenever possible? Or is it an essential right and integral part of modern litigation practice, enabling parties and courts to develop the information they need to resolve an underlying dispute?" Yablon and Lansman-Roos (2012), p. 722.

[30] Describing the arguments presented on each side, Bone emphasized that "proponents of broad discovery cite benefits for the quality of settlements and trial outcomes, for filing and other litigation incentives, and for incentives to comply with the substantive law." This would include, for example, the reduction of information asymmetry, theoretically facilitating and improving settlements. On the other hand, the author also noted that "discovery is extremely costly. The Federal Judicial Center study found that discovery consumed about half of total litigation costs for the 85% of sampled cases that had some significant discovery and about 90% of total costs for the top 5% of most expensive cases. (…) moreover, these costs have increased markedly with the advent of electronic discovery. Concerns about the cost of discovery take two forms. First, some critics focus on party incentives to engage in excessive discovery, defined as discovery beyond the point where marginal benefit equals marginal cost. Second, some critics focus on party incentives to engage in abusive discovery, defined as discovery aimed not at obtaining information, but at gaining a strategic advantage by threatening the imposition of costs." It is within this argumentative context that reform perspectives would emerge. See Bone (2012).

enacted (in 1983,[31] in 1993,[32] and in 2000[33]), seeking to incorporate principles that would render the subject proportional. Furthermore, since these modifications did not achieve the expected results,[34] a more radical change was introduced in 2015, addressing the core of the issue and aiming to fully align its regulatory treatment.[35]

With this scope, the new wording of *Rule 26(b)(1)* established that, provided there were no other limitations imposed by the Court, the discovery phase could

---

[31] "The concept of proportionality in discovery was formally incorporated into the Federal Rules of Civil Procedure in 1983. At that time, Rule 26(b)(1)(iii) was amended to 'address the problems of discovery that is proportionate to the individual lawsuit' and the perceived tendency of litigants to abuse the discovery process in order to gain a tactical advantage. The amended Rule 26 required courts to limit discovery where 'the burden or expense of the proposed discovery outweighs its likely benefit, considering the needs of the case, the amount in controversy, the parties' resources, the importance of the issues at stake in the action, and the importance of the discovery in resolving the issues.'" Laporte and Redgrave (2015), p. 22.

[32] "In 1993, further amendments to Rule 26(b)(2) added two more factors to the proportionality analysis: whether 'the burden or expense of the proposed discovery outweighs its likely benefit,' and 'the importance of the proposed discovery in resolving the issues.' The 1993 Advisory Committee Note stated that '[t]he revisions in Rule 26(b)(2) are intended to provide the court with broader discretion to impose additional restrictions on the scope and extent of discovery.' The Note also stated that the changes in Rule 26(b)(2) were designed 'to enable the court to keep tighter rein on the extent of discovery.' Although the rule change was met with some fanfare, its effect on discovery practice appears to have been muted." Laporte and Redgrave (2015), p. 29.

[33] "In 2000, the scope of discovery under Rule 26(b)(1) was finally substantively narrowed, permitting only discovery relevant to the 'claims and defenses,' and not merely the 'subject matter' of the case. A requirement of good cause was imposed for discovery beyond the new, 'refined' boundary. With the 2000 amendments to Rule 26(b)(1), the Advisory Committee acknowledged that concerns among the bench and bar over cost, delay, and general 'over-discovery' had become persistent. At the same time, the committee recognized that the new boundary would be difficult to enforce. The 'dividing line' between information relevant to the general subject matter of the case, but not to the actual claims and defenses, is difficult to draw." Netzorg and Kern (2010), p. 521.

[34] "Judicial opinions appear to confirm that little has changed since the 1983, 1993, and 2000 amendments to Rule 26(b)(1). The default rule of broad and liberal discovery remains intact. In 2010, even after all these rule amendments, the presumption continues to be that if there exists 'any possibility' that information or material is relevant to the case, 'it should generally be produced.' The resisting party continues to bear the burden of showing by specific proof why information should not be produced, whether on the basis of cost, burden, or need." Netzorg and Kern (2010), p. 522.

[35] "Finally, after four years, three hearings, and thousands of comments, the Standing Committee submitted proposed rules to the United States Judicial Conference in May of 2014. The Standing Committee was resolute that 'proportional discovery will decrease the cost of resolving disputes without sacrificing fairness.' The Standing Committee also reported that the proposed rules were 'largely unchanged from those published for public comment.' Nonetheless, the amended Rule proposal was a response to many of the commenters' concerns. In the main text of the Rule, the Committee moved 'the amount in controversy' factor from the first position, and inserted 'the importance of the issues at stake in the action' in its place. This was done to 'add prominence to the importance of the issues and avoid any implication that the amount in controversy is the most important concern.' In addition, the Committee added a new factor: 'the parties' relative access to relevant information.' This was added to 'address the reality that some cases involve an asymmetric distribution of information' and oftentimes 'one party must bear greater burdens in responding to discovery than the other party bears.'" Laporte and Redgrave (2015), pp. 39–40.

encompass any matter (relevant to the initial pleadings or the defense) that was proportional to the needs of the case.

- Once again, with this, the broad judgment of proportionality received explicit endorsement—constituting an essential test for procedural activity.

This test would specifically consider: (1) the importance of the issues at stake; (2) the value in dispute; (3) the parties' access to information, as well as the resources available to them; (4) the significance of the evidentiary production for clarifying the case; and (5) the relationship between the costs of the requested investigation and its likely benefits.[36]

Furthermore, we could mention other circumstances in which this broad proportionality has played an important role in procedural arrangements—seeking to balance its limits and necessities. In the words of Uzelac, "*most national judiciaries handle 'small' and 'big' cases; complex and routine cases; unique cases and repetitive/cloned cases. Two issues arise in this context: first, whether some types of cases are for one or the other system more 'typical'; and, second, whether or not the goals and modalities of their implementation are in each given system adjusted to the different nature of the case at hand.*" Thus providing concrete support for this assessment.[37] This underscores the importance of advocating for proportionality, aiming to bridge the gap between *books* and *reality*.

5.3 Conceptual Keys and Proportionality

Considering the benefits of this broad proportionality assessment, we believe that a primary and significant area for its application has already been previously outlined. In summary, if it has been stated that our legal process regularly seeks legitimacy through broad concepts such as the guarantees of "due process" or "participation," we believe that the interpretive guide proposed here can play an important role in reconstructing this path. Through its use, we avoid interpreting these key concepts in absolute terms, introducing a more concrete filter for their analysis.

---

[36] "26(b)(1) Unless otherwise limited by court order, the scope of discovery is as follows: Parties may obtain discovery regarding any nonprivileged matter that is relevant to any party's claim or defense and proportional to the needs of the case, considering the importance of the issues at stake in the action, the amount in controversy, the parties' relative access to relevant information, the parties' resources, the importance of the discovery in resolving the issues, and whether the burden or expense of the proposed discovery outweighs its likely benefit."

[37] See Uzelac (2012). See also Laporte and Redgrave (2015).

Indeed, following the line of authors such as Alexy[38] or Borowski,[39] it is now commonplace for readings based on absolute criteria to be rejected even in the realm of fundamental rights. The principled nature of these provisions turns them into *prima facie* optimization mandates: although their application is necessary, it is subject to a case-by-case proportionality analysis.[40] We believe that this reasoning also applies to civil procedural law.[41]

In light of this, the first implication to be drawn corresponds to what was previously referred to as intraprocedural proportionality. When we conceive procedural guarantees from this perspective, we observe that they undergo a constant process of accommodation. As mentioned, the plurality of values present within the procedural arena means that different principles of equal normative status may come into conflict. In such circumstances, their readjustment becomes necessary.

- As an example, it is common for both the concept of "adversarial proceedings" and the notion of "reasonable duration" to have fundamental status within the

[38] Analyzing the decision-making process, the author states, for example, that "this situation is not resolved by declaring that one of the two principles is invalid and eliminating it from the legal system. Nor is it resolved by introducing an exception to one of the principles in such a way that, in all future cases, this principle must be regarded as a rule that is either satisfied or not. The solution to the conflict rather consists in establishing, taking into account the circumstances of the case, a relationship of conditional precedence between the principles." Alexy (1993), pp. 91–92.

[39] See Borowski (2003).

[40] Barroso, for example, emphasizes that "fundamental rights are not absolute and, as a consequence, their exercise is subject to limitations; and, since they are generally structured as principles, fundamental rights, in many situations, are applied through balancing." Barroso (2009), p. 332. See also Barcellos (2005).

[41] Recognizing the possibility that the subject may take on different forms, Ragone points out that "this may also mean that procedural justice depends to some extent on the configuration given by the legislator to the exercise of procedural rights. The difficulty here lies in determining according to which criteria the legislator may shape the procedure or restrict the parties' freedom in exercising their procedural rights. A first consideration is to bear in mind that it is difficult for any non-utilitarian theory to set limits to these rights; in other words, every implementation of a right entails costs, generates expenses, even if these are offset by the benefits. This is why procedural rights cannot be entirely immune to efficiency calculations, since these rights are exercised within an organic-procedural framework of a public function and, therefore, there is an inherent whole to their exercise that cannot be disregarded. Thus, economic reasons, the weighing of time and money, in addition to the need for necessary deontological considerations of justice, require an assessment of the cost of limiting one procedural right in favor of another. This is where the importance of the principle or maxim of procedural economy comes into play, which is nothing more than the application of the principle to procedural rights and their limitations, whose addressee is the legislator. This is to distinguish it from procedural economy in the strict sense, or that which is addressed to the institution or body responsible for applying procedural rules to a case. In the case of judicial proceedings, the judicial body may invoke these procedural principles or maxims both as interpretative norms and as standards for admitting or denying a particular procedural alternative. No one disputes the role of effectiveness and efficiency, for example, in the actions of the public administration within the course of administrative proceedings, based on the need for an adequate distribution of the State's scarce resources. In our case, this postulate is also applicable, but in relation to the resources of the Judiciary, which require limiting or expanding the exercise of certain rights in the proceedings." Ragone (2014), p. 257.

same legal system. Given the inherent tension between the two, one might question whether, in analyzing a particular case, it would be appropriate to deny effect to one and protect only the opposing principle.[42] In our view, the answer is negative. By rejecting the absolute nature of either of these principles, their ongoing process of accommodation and balancing is justified. One side may tend to prevail, but without excluding the opposing side from the balance of interests.[43]

Once again, however, we believe that there is ample opportunity to bring the broader dimension of proportionality into consideration. From this second perspective, it becomes necessary for the concepts of procedure to be shaped not only in response to their potential internal conflicts but also to the cultural and structural factors that surround them.

- This gives rise to a new range of questions. For example, from a globally proportional perspective, is it appropriate for any legal regime to coexist with an individual interpretation of the right of action? Is it required or advisable that any procedural system should fully recognize the possibility of participation in court?

As demonstrated in the previous section, this interpretation is also facilitated by resorting to comparative analysis. In this way, we observe that, similarly, the present proposal is materially supported, constituting a path already established on different scales.

---

[42] Examining this *trade-off* and proposing some solution for its configuration, Dinamarco points out that, in contemporary jurisdiction, "the most serious problem is the *duration of proceedings*, which leads to the *perpetuation* of disputes and prolongs the distress of litigants. However, it will never be possible to expedite procedures *so much* that, in general, they are able to provide a sufficiently prompt resolution to disputes (…) there are certain legitimate reasons in favor of lengthy proceedings, such as the mutual security of the parties, guarantees of defense, and adversarial process (…) this means that every effort to expedite proceedings encounters limits (…) which lead the system's architect to accept the rational balance possible between two antagonistic requirements, namely: on the one hand, *procedural celerity*, which aims to achieve pacification as soon as possible; on the other, *deliberation in handling the case* and the parties' arguments (…) an examination of the basic features of the judicial process in its operational design (procedure, opportunity for defense, appeals, etc.) reveals the indispensable coexistence between rules aimed at expediting it and rules that prevent excessive acceleration, requiring greater *deliberation* in the handling of disputes." Dinamarco (2005), pp. 160–161.

[43] In identifying this latent conflict, Teori Albino Zavascki argues that the issue should be resolved (both at the legislative level and within the judiciary) through a careful application of the proportionality test and its evaluative parameters. In his words, "since these are fundamental rights of identical constitutional origin, there is no hierarchy, at the normative level, between the right to effective judicial protection and the right to legal certainty, and both must therefore receive the strictest and most faithful observance from both the ordinary legislator and the judge. However, as with other fundamental rights, tensions may also arise between these rights in practice. There is, in fact, a factual element particularly apt to trigger such tensions: the factor of *time*. The passage of time, as everyone knows, is often incompatible with the effectiveness of judicial protection (…) whenever a situation arises in which the right to legal certainty cannot coexist harmoniously and simultaneously with the right to effective judicial protection, there will be a case of collision between the fundamental rights of the litigants, requiring a harmonizing solution." Zavascki (2009), pp. 67–68.

To illustrate this point, we believe that the main example is provided by the concept of "due process." This concept is regarded by theorists as central to contemporary civil procedure, assuming a prominent role in its structure. However, we also consider that, even in establishing this standard, one cannot disregard the complex context formed by substantive limits, which requires that its interpretation be carried out in a proportional manner.

To begin this overview, it can be stated that the logic of "due process" originated in England, with the purpose of preventing any individual from suffering harm to their life, liberty, or property without observance of the local law ("*law of the land*").[44] It thus had a distinctly restrictive character regarding State action,[45] a negative order, in line with the prevailing mentality of the period and seeking to prevent interference in the private sphere.[46] Consequently, its content was primarily procedural ("*procedural due process*")—aiming to establish minimum barriers to public intervention in the individual sphere.[47]

Alongside this provision, it also gradually became common to invoke the idea of "due process" to designate a new order of limitation on the public sphere—of a substantive nature ("*substantial due process*"). From this perspective, the guarantee began to acquire substantive content, seeking to inhibit state intervention and initially favoring a *laissez-faire* logic.[48] According to a jurisprudential position that persisted for decades, Public Administration would always be required to

---

[44] According to the wording of the Magna Carta, dated 1215, "nullus liber homo capiatur, vel imprisonetur, aut disseisiatur, aut utlagetur, aut exulatur, aut aliquo modo destruatur, nec super eum ibimus, nec super eum mittemus, nisi per legale judicium parium suorum vel per legum terre" ("no free man shall be seized or imprisoned, or exiled, or in any way destroyed (…) except by the lawful judgment of his peers or by the law of the land"). Thus, it can be seen that in its original formulation, the guarantee was not expressly labeled as "due process." See Wasserman (2004).

[45] "The concept of due process emerges from the central paradox in the creation of state authority. As framed in the American Constitution, for example, the due process command is directed as a negative limitation on what the state may do to the citizenry." Issacharoff (2005), p. 2.

[46] Note, however, that according to Sunstein, this point could be interpreted in two ways: (1) on the one hand, "due process of law" would indeed represent a protection of the individual against the State; (2) on the other hand, it could constitute a prerogative of the State vis-à-vis the individual. In this latter logic, the guarantee would not prevent the state entity from disturbing the individual, instead serving a permissive and precisely opposite function: such disturbance would be permissible and authorized as long as it complied with the "law of the land." Thus, quoting Justice Scalia's dissenting opinion in *Lawrence v. Texas*, Sunstein highlights the following statement by the Justice: "there is no right to 'liberty' under the Due Process Clause (…) The Fourteenth Amendment expressly allows states to deprive their citizens of 'liberty,' so long as 'due process of law' is provided." Commenting on this view, Sunstein states that "fundamentalists don't believe that the Constitution protects the right to privacy. In their view, government has no general duty to respect people's choices about how to conduct their private lives." See Sunstein (2005), p. 81.

[47] Orth (2003), pp. 15–26.

[48] On the close relationship between *economic substantive due process*, particularly as established in the *Lochner* case, and the economic policy of *laissez-faire*, see Lindsay (2010).

demonstrate that its intervention was adequate, fair, and appropriate—thus imposing a heavy burden of justification.[49]

In any case, returning to the dimension of the guarantee that concerns us, comparative analysis shows that over the decades its application to procedural law has undergone significant changes (largely attributable to the activity of the courts themselves[50]). This evolution ultimately incorporated a broad proportionality assessment similar to the one proposed here, seeking to align civil procedure with its real possibilities and to make it more functional.[51]

As commonly noted in legal scholarship, this shift reached its apex with the 1976 decision of the United States Supreme Court in Mathews v. Eldridge. Until then, a broader and more theoretical notion of "due process" had prevailed; however, on that occasion, the Court expressly established the following: "due process, unlike some legal rules, is not a technical conception with a fixed content unrelated to time, place, and circumstances." It would be "flexible and calls for such procedural protections as the particular situation demands."

Breaking down this concern, three general factors have been identified as responsible for shaping the notion of "due process": "Due process generally requires consideration of three distinct factors: First, the private interest that will be affected by the official action; second, the risk of an erroneous deprivation of such interest through the procedures used, and the probable value, if any, of additional or substitute procedural safeguards; and finally, the Government's interest, including the function involved and the fiscal and administrative burdens that the additional or substitute procedural requirement would entail." Based on this, it is not possible to conceive of "due process" as an absolute guarantee afforded to the party, but rather as a scalable filter,[52] as a flexible criterion to be proportionally established according to the general circumstances surrounding the case.

---

[49] According to the Supreme Court, establishing the "Lochner test," which gained notoriety and served as a guide for jurisprudence throughout much of the twentieth century, the question to be examined in assessing the legality of conduct under substantive due process was as follows: "is this a fair, reasonable and appropriate exercise of the police power of the State, or is it an unreasonable, unnecessary and arbitrary interference with the right of the individual to his personal liberty (...)?" It should also be noted that this position was later revised, essentially as a result of a power struggle in which the Judiciary yielded. As Orth explains, "President Franklin Roosevelt (...) began, and launched a remarkable assault on the Supreme Court of the United States (...) within days, the president's supporters in Congress introduced the Court Reform bill, better known as the 'court-packing plan,' designed to secure an economic majority of justices to uphold the government's economic program (...) Roosevelt's Court Reform bill was never adopted, foundering on a public consensus that it would have too obviously politicized the judicial branch. But a majority of the sitting justices rather suddenly coalesced in support of the president's program, abandoning economic substantive due process." Orth (2003), pp. 67–69.

[50] "In a system based on precedent, nothing is ever truly lost. The history of the law of due process, marked by the succession of paradigm cases, has been accretive: new paradigms have added to the content of the law." Orth (2003), p. 85.

[51] Issacharoff (2005), pp. 5–9.

[52] "One way of understanding due process is as an affirmative entitlement of the citizenry. Under this view (...) citizens may be thought of as having a right to a hearing and a right to notice, such

- The construction presented above demonstrates that, on that occasion, the realization of "due process" was conditioned upon a proportionality analysis analogous to the one proposed here. The danger of absolutizing the guarantee was recognized, as well as the need to adapt it to the demands and possibilities of the real world.

Given this background and considering the cultural nature of civil procedure, it is appropriate here to raise questions similar to those previously mentioned: how has this type of thinking been applied? Is there, in Western procedure, an open use of this kind of approach?

In our view, this type of more critical reasoning still seems even more distant from the continental legal environment. As a result, at the risk of distancing *books* from reality, we overlook an important observation made by Owen Fiss: "*due process requires that procedures be fair, but fairness is a pragmatic ideal; it affords protection to the individual, but not in a way that would require the sacrifice of other important rights.*"[53]

It is certain that these reinterpretations must be read in light of our own context and its particularities.[54] In any case, the issue here also appears to be the same: regardless of the concept, it is essential to be aware of its place within the complexities of the proceedings, understanding it in a coherent and proportionate manner.[55]

---

that they can claim 'ownership' of these against any type of adverse governmental action. Alternatively, due process may be characterized not as vesting the citizens with rights, but as imposing restraints on the state. Seen this way, due process is a check against arbitrary, capricious, or simply misguided conduct. And in addition, under this view, there might be gradations in terms of how fixed the requirements of due process are thought to be, or of whether they are more in the nature of prudential checks against mistake." Issacharoff (2005), p. 6.

[53] Fiss (1993), p. 979.

[54] In this regard, it is worth noting that, in Brazil, there are authors who seek to replace the very notion of "due process" with that of a "fair trial." This is the case of Daniel Mitidiero, who states: "The Constitution refers to due process of law (*due process of law*). The expression is subject to criticism on at least two fronts. First, because it refers to the cultural context of the Rule of Law (*Rechtsstaat, État Légal*), in which the procedural system was conceived solely as a safeguard against state arbitrariness, whereas today the Constitutional State (*Verfassungsstaat, État de Droit*) is tasked with contributing to the effective protection of rights through the organization of a fair trial. Second, because it gives rise, due to the American tradition from which it was borrowed, to the search for a substantive dimension to the provision (*substantive due process of law*), when there is no need to consider it beyond its procedural dimension in Brazilian law." Based on this, he concludes that "these are the reasons why the doctrine prefers to speak of the right to a fair trial (*giusto processo, procès équitable, faires Verfahren, fair trial*)—in addition to being culturally consistent with the Constitutional State, this immediately reveals the purely procedural nature of its content. The right to a fair trial is a minimum model for structuring the judicial process (…) it is the task of all those committed to the rule of the Constitutional State to outline and develop it." Mitidiero (2011), p. 22.

[55] In this regard, however, it is worth noting Tamanaha's caveat when analyzing the dangers inherent in a belief in the primacy of the *rule of law* in its formalist sense. According to the author, "the thin conception of the rule of law does not impose any requirements concerning the content of the law. This openness with respect to content renders the rule of law amenable to all sorts of cultures, societies and political systems. It does not specify the kinds of law a society must have, nor does it

This reasoning could also be applied to other conceptual keys incorporated into the discipline in the form of guarantees. In summary, given the indeterminacy of these parameters, their definition requires ongoing interpretive work. Moreover, this hermeneutic approach must not disregard the concrete needs and limitations of judicial activity.

- To clarify this point, we can take as an example the role played in the procedural framework by the concept of "adversarial proceedings"—also referred to under other labels such as the right to "participation," the right to "be heard," or the right to a "day in court." In all these cases, the minimum underlying requirement appears to be the same, namely, the opportunity for a party to participate in the proceedings and influence the decision. Here as well, we consider that the concept should be understood with certain reservations, applying it with a sense of proportionality.

It is in this context, for example, that the argument is made for allowing representation to take precedence over personal participation in court proceedings. Essentially, this latter approach would permit an individual to be bound by a decision even without having personally participated in the proceedings, provided that their interests were adequately represented therein. This reversal is advocated by authors such as Fiss,[56] and may represent an important step toward procedural

indicate any particular limits on the law. It requires only that government officials and citizens be bound by and act in accordance with the law, whatever the law might require. This also means that oppressive or immoral rules can be enacted—for example, imposing slavery, apartheid and religious or caste distinctions—without falling foul of the requirements of the rule of law." Thus, Tamanaha (2009), p. 13.

[56]The issue is thoroughly addressed by Fiss in his analysis of the case *Martin v. Wilkins*, in which the substantive matter concerned the possible adoption of protective measures to promote the professional advancement of Black firefighters. On that occasion, the main debate before the courts was not the merits of the proposal itself, but rather whether it could be implemented without guaranteeing a "day in court" for the white firefighters—since its implementation would cause them concrete harm. Based on this circumstance, and although this was not the prevailing interpretation in the case, Fiss argued that the true guarantee to be ensured for the protection of material interests should not be one of *participation*, but of *representation*. Consequently, it would be incorrect to categorically state that a decision could not bind individuals who had not participated in the proceedings. In fact, the more appropriate idea would be that "no individual could be bound by a decision unless his or her interest had been adequately represented" in court. Explaining this issue, Fiss noted: "Let us further assume that this decree is subsequently attacked by persons such as the white firefighters who were not parties to the case but who will be adversely affected by the decree. They claim that the system of preferential treatment is a form of unjust discrimination and thus unconstitutional. In passing on this claim, the trial court might be constrained by considerations of stare decisis but not, according to Martin v. Wilks, by the tougher preclusion rules of res judicata and collateral estoppel. The trial court would have to give the white firefighters a full hearing on their claim even though, before entering the decree, the court had already concluded that such preferences were constitutional, indeed necessary, to correct for the past violations." And, in light of this, he concluded: "Of course, we might have to live with these consequences if the right of participation were constitutionally grounded, but that is far from clear. I believe that what the Constitution guarantees is not a right of participation, but rather what I will call a 'right of repre-

effectiveness. In the words of Clermont, it is a matter of choosing a realistic and reasonable criterion.[57]

Once again, however, this type of reasoning also does not seem to be fully present in continental reality—creating a gap between theory and practice that any more critical analysis should seek to narrow. Although its plural nature allows the discipline to operate in different ways, the complexity of the underlying issues cannot be overlooked.

In concluding this chapter, we further emphasize that, in our view, this same broad assessment of proportionality would represent a significant advancement in the interpretation of other indeterminate concepts in dispute resolution, such as "reasonable duration." In summary, it is also pertinent to ask here: can this *acceleration* be considered in isolation? Is it reasonable to advocate for it without taking into account its material feasibility?

We consider the answers to be negative. Approaching the procedural system critically means recognizing its argumentative and flexible nature, seeking to align it with its real possibilities. In this reconstruction, the principle of proportionality can play an important role.

References

Alexy, R. (1993). *Teoria de los derechos fundamentales*. Centro de Estudios Constitucionales.

Andrews, N. (2012). *The three paths of justice: Courts proceedings, arbitration and mediation in England*. Springer.

Arenhart, S. C. (2013). *A tutela coletiva de interesses individuais: para além da proteção dos interesses individuais homogêneos*. Ed. RT.

Arenhart, S. C., & Osna, G. (2014). Complexity, proportionality and the 'pan-procedural' approach: Some bases of contemporary civil litigation. *International Journal of Procedural Law,* 4.

Barcellos, A. P. (2005). *Ponderação, racionalidade e atividade jurisdicional*. Renovar.

Barroso, L. R. (2009). *Curso de Direito Constitucional Contemporâneo*. Saraiva.

Bone, R. G. (2012). Discovery. In C. W. Sanchirico (Ed.), *Procedural law and economics*. Edward Elgar.

Borowski, M. (2003). *La estructura de los derechos fundamentales*. Universidad Externado de Colômbia.

Caponi, R. (2011). O princípio da proporcionalidade na justiça civil. *Revista de Processo,* 192.

Carroll, J. L. (2010). Proportionality in discovery: A cautionary tale. *Campbell Law Review*, 32.

Clermont, K. M. (2005). *Principles of civil procedure*. Thomson West.

Cooter, R., & Ulen, T. (2000). *Law & economics* (3rd ed.). Addison Wesley Longman.

sentation': not a day in court but the right to have one's interest adequately represented." See Fiss (1993), pp. 969–972.

[57] "Binding absentees does not contravene the Constitution, because all that due process guarantees is a full and fair day in court enjoyed in person *or through a representative* (…) Therefore, the always reasonable and realistic due process test allows binding many more nonparties than most people assume." Clermont (2005), p. 387.

Cunha, A. (2010). Os desafios ao Estado, à governança e à gestão pública: explorando ideias para subsidiar os esforços de reforma da gestão nas organizações do Poder Judiciário. In J. R. Cunha (Ed.), *Poder Judiciário: Novos Olhares sobre Gestão e Jurisdição*. Editora FGV.
Dinamarco, C. R. (2005). *Instituições de Direito Processual Civil* (Vol. 1). Malheiros.
Fiss, O. (1993). The allure of individualism. *Iowa Law Review*, 78.
Frankfurter, H. G. (2015). *On inequality*. Princeton University Press.
Issacharoff, S. (2005). *Civil procedure*. Foundation Press.
Kornhausen, L. (2012). Judicial organization and administration. In C. W. Sanchirico (Ed.), *Procedural law and economics*. Edward Elgar.
Laporte, E. D., & Redgrave, J. M. (2015). A practical guide to achieving proportionality under new federal rule of civil procedure. *The Federal Courts Law Review, 26*, 9.
Lindsay, M. J. (2010). In Search of 'Laissez-Faire Constitutionalism'. *Harvard Law Review Forum*, 123.
Miceli, T. J. (2012). The social versus private incentive to sue. In C. W. Sanchirico (Ed.), *Procedural law and economics*. Edward Elgar.
Mitidiero, D. (2011). Direito Fundamental ao Processo Justo. *Revista Magister de Direito Civil e Processual Civil*, 45.
Netzorg, G. W., & Kern, T. D. (2010). Proportional discovery: Making it the norm, rather than the exception. *Denver University Law Review*, 87.
Orth, J. V. (2003). *Due process of law – A brief history*. University Press of Kansas.
Osna, G. (2012). Entre a Teoria e a Concretização - Possibilidades, Limites e Funções para uma Nova Lei de Imprensa. *Revista do Instituto dos Advogados do Paraná*, 41.
Ragone, A. P. (2014). Retrato del revisionismo garantista en el proceso civil a través de Klein y Wach. *Revista de Processo*, 233.
Ragone, A. P. (2016). La revalorización de la audiencia preliminar o preparatoria: una mirada desde la justicia distributiva en el proceso civil. *Revista de Processo*, 252.
Shavell, S. (1982). The social versus the private incentive to bring suit in a costly legal system. *The Journal of Legal Studies*, 11.
Silva, V. A. (2002). O proporcional e o razoável. *Revista dos Tribunais*, 798.
Sunstein, C. R. (2005). *Radical in Robes – Why extreme right-wing courts are wrong for America?* Perseus Books Group.
Tamanaha, B. Z. (2009). A concise guide to the rule of law. In G. Palombella & N. Walker (Eds.), *Relocating the rule of law*. Hart.
Timm, L. B. (2008). Qual a maneira mais eficiente de prover direitos fundamentais: uma perspectiva de direito e economia? In L. B. Timm & I. W. Sarlet (Eds.), *Direitos Fundamentais: orçamento e reserva do possível*. Livraria do Advogado.
Uzelac, A. (2012). Goals of civil justice and civil procedure in the contemporary world. In A. Uzelac (Ed.), *Goals of civil justice and civil procedure in contemporary judicial systems*. Springer.
Wasserman, R. (2004). *Procedural due process – A reference guide to the American constitution*. Praeger.
Yablon, C., & Lansman-Roos, N. (2012). Discovery about discovery: Sampling practice and the resolution of discovery disputes in an age of ever-increasing information. *Cardozo Law Review*, 34.
Zavascki, T. A. (2009). *Antecipação da Tutela* (7th ed.). Saraiva.
Zuckerman, A. (1996). Lord Woolf's access to justice: Plus a change. *The Modern Law Review*, 59.

Chapter 6
Reimagining Civil Procedure: Possibilities and Alternatives

6.1 Alternative Dispute Resolution Methods

With the path established throughout this work, we seek to provide the reader with a new foundation for understanding civil procedure. A more critical perspective, interpreting its characteristics and elements from a viewpoint distinct from the traditional one. In this chapter, we aim to conclude the study by highlighting specific areas in which this new approach can play a significant role. The first of these is the field of alternative dispute resolution (ADR).

Beginning this investigation, it is important to note that, under this conceptual umbrella, a wide range of dispute resolution methods distinct from the official mechanism emerges.[1] The notion of "alternative" serves to designate the non-coincidence between the mechanism of dispute resolution and state jurisdiction; it is established as the rule, with all other avenues considered exceptions.

In light of this context, we begin the current discussion from a slightly different premise. As noted at the outset of this work, state centralization represented a political choice—structured at a particular historical moment and persisting ever since. It is not the only correct path, but merely one of the various ways in which the resolution of disputes could be shaped.

[1] The issue is raised (and problematized) by Ian Macneil, who notes: "the fact that little is really new in ADR is obscured by the very phrase, Alternative Dispute Resolution. The word alternative means alternative to dispute resolution processes of the State – the judges, juries, administrative dispute resolvers, and the like of the State legal system. Thus the term ADR presupposes that the primary, fundamental dispute resolution system is that provided by the State, alternative methods being secondary, supplemental, and probably suspect. This statist view of dispute resolution simply turns the world upside down, whether we look to history or to present socioeconomic behavior. Historically the truly *alternative* dispute resolution methods are those of State law. State law is the Johnny-come-lately on the scene, because the State itself is a relatively recent development." Macneil (1992), pp. 03–04.

G. Osna, *Civil Procedure, Culture, and Proportionality*,
https://doi.org/10.1007/978-3-032-27555-4_6

Thus, upon critical analysis, there is nothing to prevent techniques that are regarded as alternative in our system from assuming predominance in another context.[2] In fact, considering that the monopolistic advance of the State has not always been present, submitting every conflict to its analysis has not always been the first (or only) option. It was with the affirmation of liberal values that this idea emerged, seeking to avoid social institutions outside the public sphere.

Furthermore, it is important to emphasize that the scope of this notion of alternative means is uncontrollable—there is no way to enumerate all the para-state mechanisms capable of resolving a dispute. From a condominium meeting to a parent intervening in a quarrel between children, various forms of conflict resolution are brought into play. In short, disputes are inevitable in any society, and the different possibilities for their resolution cannot be fully encompassed by theoretical discourse.

However, for the present purposes, we intend to limit our analysis to two elements regularly included in this framework: self-composition, through conciliation or mediation, and arbitral adjudication. Although both aspects are often addressed under the same umbrella, we consider that distinguishing between them is essential.

We begin our analysis with the first aspect, related to the concepts of mediation and conciliation. Here, although the two notions have relevant differences,[3] they

---

[2] "ADR has become so diverse in its processes and dispute arenas that professionals are endeavoring to coordinate and make sense of these various efforts (…) as ADR developed and expanded, practitioners began to change how they looked at it, even questioning its name. For some practitioners, the courts are really the alternative dispute settlement process, suggesting that 'ADR' represents the usual conflict resolution processes. Others have suggested that the 'A' in ADR should stand for appropriate, since in ADR the parties choose the process they feel is most appropriate for their needs and interests. Still others say conflict resolution (CR) should replace ADR. Others offer collaborative problem solving (CPR) as the better term." Barrett and Barrett (2004), pp. 256–257.

[3] As noted by Daniela Gabbay, "it is important to emphasize that there are significant differences to be considered between mediation, conciliation, and negotiation. Between the first two and negotiation, there is a formal distinction in the presence of a neutral third party (mediator or conciliator), since negotiation is bilateral and involves only the parties themselves in reaching an agreement. This is the difference between direct self-composition (negotiation) and assisted self-composition (mediation and conciliation). The substantive distinctions between conciliation and mediation concern the manner and qualifications of the third party's involvement, the degree of control exercised over the process, the type of conflict, and the relationship between the parties—factors that directly influence the objectives of self-compositional techniques. Regarding the third party's role, it may be more or less active (…) with conciliators generally being more active and directive during the session, and even able to propose settlement ideas to the parties (…) in conciliation, the procedure is simpler and the session quicker, as the merits of the case are usually not addressed, with the focus directed toward reaching an agreement, whereas in mediation, agreement is not the goal but merely one possible outcome (…) the conciliator may assume a position of authority (…) in the conciliation session, which differs from the role assumed by the mediator in the mediation session, where the parties themselves take center stage and bear responsibility for resolving the dispute." Gabbay (2013), pp. 47–49.

both share the same core element: the fact that the individuals themselves establish a means of resolving the dispute.[4]

- The change is clear, breaking away from the classical structure of the proceedings. While in the judicial sphere, the need to choose a third party is paramount, resulting in an act of authority, in this parallel process, such intervention becomes unnecessary. If the conflict is between "A" and "B," it is they themselves who should seek the best solution.

Far from being a novelty, this form of dispute resolution is culturally grounded and has anthropological roots, engaging with the social environment in which it operates.[5] Thus, mediation or conciliation is more likely to be adopted within groups inclined toward dialogue and solidarity. This is both because, in such circumstances, external adjudication is less necessary (given the sense of community) and due to the ongoing nature of relationships (making rifts undesirable).[6] Aware that they

---

[4] "A third form of ADR moves even further away from formal methods of information development. Conversation (sometimes referred to as mediation, sometimes as a conference, sometimes as evaluation) is used to elicit agreement between the parties. Judge-led settlement conferences are an example of this type of ADR, as are 'early neutral evaluations' ('ENE'). In this form of ADR, the relationship between information and outcome may be unclear, partly due to the lack of formal articulation by the third party of its views on the respective positions of the disputants. Reaching agreement is one objective, as is narrowing the dispute, should further proceedings or adjudication be necessary. When settlements occur, it is due to the parties' consent, which may or may not reflect their legal rights." Resnik (1995), p. 220.

[5] "This imagined story of prehistoric times illustrates that while humans have always had the tendency to resolve their differences through conflict, they have also recognized the benefits of settling matters peacefully, whether by flipping a coin or by other means. This search for alternatives to violence gave rise to the precursors of alternative dispute resolution (ADR). The most basic form of ADR is negotiation: at its core, two people simply discuss a problem and attempt to reach a mutually acceptable resolution. Mediation, therefore, began when two negotiators, realizing they needed assistance, accepted the intervention of a third party. If the third party was asked to make a decision or if the decision was left to some arbitrary mechanism, the process became arbitration (…) ADR is often regarded as a new method of resolving disputes. In reality, its roots run deep in human history, and it has long played a crucial role in cultures around the world. To trace the origins of ADR, we can turn to anthropological and sociological studies of traditional societies for insight into some of the ways early humans may have resolved disputes without resorting to fists, clubs, or poison arrows. Many of these conflict resolution methods are strikingly foreign to our Western perspective. Nevertheless, they have much to teach us about the value of conflict in airing everyday disagreements and how to use them as opportunities to deepen relationships and achieve lasting harmony." Barrett and Barrett (2004), pp. 01–02.

[6] Identifying this dialogue in the historical experience of the United States, Auerbach highlights that "historically, arbitration and mediation (…) expressed an ideology of community justice without formal law, an equitable process based on reciprocity and trust among community members. They emerged as native forms of self-government. The communities that rejected the judicial means of dispute resolution were highly diverse, with different geographic, ideological, religious, ethnic, and even commercial characteristics. Yet, their unity of vision is remarkable. Despite their diversity, they used identical processes because they shared a common commitment to the essence of community life: reciprocity, responsibility, and trust. The founders of Dedham (a seventeenth-century Christian utopian community in Massachusetts), the early Quakers of Philadelphia, the followers of John Humphrey Noyes in Oneida (a nineteenth-century utopian commune), the

would continue to depend on one another, the parties should resolve their differences as soon as possible and preferably without producing losers.

Alongside this hypothesis, the discourse on alternative dispute resolution methods also consistently moves toward the presentation and defense of the arbitration institute. The difference here is fundamental: whereas in mediation and conciliation the central idea is that the parties themselves resolve their conflict, in arbitration the decision-making act is delegated to a third party.

Understanding this premise, we realize that arbitral proceedings do not differ in structure from traditional civil proceedings. In both cases, the dispute is resolved through heterocomposition. In other words, it is up to an impartial party to analyze its nuances and determine its outcome.[7]

However, the fundamental difference between the two fields lies in the authority responsible for the decision: in its official framework, the discipline falls within the scope of the State, whereas with arbitration, the resolution may be shifted away from this sector; in the face of an existing or potential dispute, the parties may choose to submit its resolution to a private individual.[8] This establishes a consensus regarding the dissent: the parties disagree on the merits of the dispute, but agree on the most appropriate forum to resolve it.

Chinese in San Francisco, the Scandinavians in Minnesota, and even businessmen from a Chamber of Commerce could easily have collaborated in developing a common project for dispute resolution. Sharing a suspicion of lawyers and laws, they developed conflict resolution standards that reflected their common struggle for social harmony beyond individual conflicts, for justice without law." Auerbach (2007), p. 44.

[7] "While the current vocabulary of ADR could enable a lengthy discussion of distinctions among processes now called arbitration, court-annexed arbitration, mediation, med-arb, mini-trial, summary jury trial, early neutral evaluation, and judicial settlement conferences,[31] all of these forms involve the state's introduction to the disputants of a third party, who is called upon to do something (…) A first mode is quasi-adjudicatory; this form of ADR offers a truncated, abbreviated fact-finding process that yields an outcome, decided by a third party, in the hopes that with that result, the parties will conclude their dispute. Both private contractual and court-annexed arbitration fit this mode. The difference is that under contractual arbitration, individuals or entities have an agreement, predating a dispute, to arbitrate, and that agreement also specifies the mechanism for selection of arbitrators. What makes this process not adjudication is that the proceeding is not conducted by a state-employed individual who bears the title "judge," formal evidentiary rules do not apply, and opinions are often not written. It is, however, important to keep in mind that this process shares with adjudication a commitment to a case-specific outcome made by a third party and predicated upon an inquiry into the claims of fact made by disputants." Resnik (1995), pp. 218–219.

[8] On this subject, Marinoni, Arenhart, and Mitidiero state that "arbitration emerges as an alternative form of dispute resolution, positioned alongside traditional jurisdiction. Its main feature lies in the attempt to circumvent the often excessive formalism of traditional proceedings, seeking a more agile mechanism for resolving issues. Moreover, arbitration can provide a path to more suitable solutions for many concrete litigation scenarios. Indeed, the fact that the arbitrator may be a professional from a field other than law can contribute to a more appropriate and precise decision. In matters that require specific expertise in a given area, it is generally much more appropriate for a decision to be rendered by a specialist in that field than by a judge who, even when assisted by an expert, does not possess in-depth knowledge of the subject or is unfamiliar with the particularities and practices of a specific situation." Marinoni et al. (2015), p. 461.

- In these terms, the core of dispute resolution through arbitration lies in the fact that the parties freely choose a third party to settle the conflict,[9] undertaking to be bound by their decision. There is, therefore, a form of waiver of state jurisdiction.[10]

For this reason, in a statistical context, it is not surprising that the institution is viewed with a critical eye—being subject to both subjective requirements and objective parameters.[11] In this way, the aim is to preserve its integrity and control the scope of its activities.[12]

---

[9] Presenting the issue, Fouchard, Gaillard, and Goldman emphasize that "arbitration should be defined by reference to two constituent elements which commentators and the courts almost unanimously recognize. First, the arbitrators' task is to resolve a dispute. Second, the source of this judicial role is a contract: the arbitrators' power to decide a dispute originates in the common intention of the parties. Thus, arbitration comprises both a judicial (§ 1) and a contractual element (§ 2)." Fouchard et al. (1999), p. 11.

[10] "The most obvious *fora* for all disputes are natural courts. They exist and are maintained by the state to provide a dispute settlement service for parties. It is a manifestation of state power and the responsibility of the state to ensure that courts exist, that appropriately qualified judges are appointed, that there are procedural rules to regulate the basis of jurisdiction and the conduct of cases before the court. Arbitration is not a national court procedure. When parties agree to arbitration they remove their relationships and disputes from the jurisdiction of national courts. There are many reasons for parties to decide that their disputes should be resolved other than in the national courts." Lew et al. (2003), p. 04.

[11] The first, referred to as "subjective arbitrability," concerns the personal conditions required for the parties to a given dispute to bind its resolution to arbitration. This reflects the contractual nature of the matter itself: as a legal transaction, this arrangement would also depend on requirements related to its agents. The adoption of this alternative route presupposes a valid agreement, entered into by parties who are capable of being bound by it. The second level of assessment, which constitutes "objective arbitrability," limits the subject matter that may be submitted to arbitral jurisdiction. This issue arises from the fact that we live in an environment marked by the centrality of the state: given the public function of safeguarding fundamental rights, the alternative method can only be applied to matters that the state, acting as judge, does not deem necessary to reserve for itself. In our current structure, this prerogative is limited to available interests of a pecuniary nature, thus preventing the field from being subject to distortions. Explaining the issue, Carmona emphasizes that "a *sine qua non* condition for the use of arbitration is the capacity of the contracting parties, without which the arbitration agreement cannot be concluded (…) considering that the establishment of arbitral jurisdiction presupposes the availability of the right, those who have only powers of administration over the asset cannot initiate arbitral proceedings," but also that "capacity alone is not sufficient to submit a dispute to arbitrators: it is also necessary that the disagreement concerns an available pecuniary right," highlighting that "arbitrable, therefore, are those cases that deal with matters for which the state does not create a specific reservation in order to protect the fundamental interests of the community, and provided that the parties are free to dispose of the asset in dispute." In the same vein, Lew, Mistelis, and Kröll note that "arbitrability is one of the issues where the contractual and jurisdictional natures of international commercial arbitration meet head on. It involves the simple question of what types of issues can and cannot be submitted to arbitration (…) national laws often impose restrictions or limitation on what matters can be referred to and resolved by arbitration." See, thus, Carmona (2009), pp. 37–39. Lew et al. (2003), p. 187.

[12] Summarizing this scope, Fouchard, Gaillard, and Goldman state that "an arbitration agreement to be effective (…) must be the result of the valid consent of the parties. However, it must also be

At this point, however, some questions may be raised: if arbitration is also fundamentally based on heterocomposition, what justifies its use? Why would the parties choose to submit the dispute to a decision-making body other than the Judiciary?

Broadly speaking, the theoretical response to these issues is closely linked to the very origins of the institution: whereas judicial proceedings are characterized by generalism,[13] arbitration allows the dispute to be resolved based on technical and specific parameters.[14] While in the state sphere, the decision is vaguely transferred to the public domain, in arbitral proceedings, it is possible to select, in a highly personalized manner, the individual responsible for rendering the decision. This ensures the expertise of the ruling, creating a favorable environment for disputes of high complexity.

In this context, mechanisms such as mediation, conciliation, and arbitration could play significant roles in our social landscape. However, when we examine the subject critically, we believe that the recent growth of these mechanisms is not a result of their specific characteristics. In fact, it reflects the broader crisis of jurisdiction itself.

From this perspective, alternative dispute resolution methods are no longer seen as merely complementary to traditional civil proceedings, but rather as genuine

---

lawful. This means, first, that the agreement must relate to subject-matter which is capable of being resolved by arbitration and, second, that the agreement must have been entered into by parties entitled to submit their disputes to arbitration. These considerations are referred to under the heading of arbitrability, and are founded upon the protection of the general interest." Fouchard et al. (1999), p. 312.

[13] "The legal structure naturally entails the appointment of generalist judges, who are once again considered 'fit' to handle diverse situations. On the other hand, the desirability of specialized judges in equally specialized courts is plausible. (…) To clarify the previous discussion, let us take specialization in medicine as an example. When visiting an orthopedic clinic, one expects to be treated by an orthopedist who, possessing a high degree of specialization, is capable of identifying and, potentially, curing a condition. However, when there is uncertainty regarding the appropriate medical specialty, one consults a general practitioner who, despite broad medical knowledge, will be limited to providing a preliminary diagnosis and will generally refer the patient to a specialist. An orthopedic clinic is incompatible with a general practitioner, and the reverse is also true. The preceding analysis reflects the structure of the American judiciary and applies appropriately and without obstacles to our own, provided the necessary precautions are observed." Lazari et al. (2013), pp. 419–420.

[14] "It is essential to highlight the qualitative difference between jurisdiction and arbitration. While arbitration may be preferred for involving arbitrators with expertise in specific techniques related to certain disputes—whose decision-making legitimacy derives from the autonomy of the parties, in addition to being confidential and faster—it must not be overlooked that jurisdiction is characterized, among other aspects, by the rules of investiture, non-delegability, and the natural judge, whose validity is grounded in state sovereignty and compliance with constitutional norms." Marinoni et al. (2015a), p. 175. See also, Marinoni et al. (2015b).

outlets for their replacement.[15] Their advancement would not result from their own inherent potential, but from the shortcomings of traditional civil procedure.[16]

In this regard, we consider that there is a constant guiding principle shaping the behavior of individuals, either encouraging or discouraging recourse to judicial activity. The lower the interest in resorting to the Judiciary, the greater the propensity to seek arbitration.[17] Conversely, the more favorable the insistence on litigation, the lower the likelihood of reaching a common ground.[18] Consequently, factors such as costs or delays in the judicial system would serve as a driving force for recourse to alternative avenues.[19]

[15] In this regard, Resnik states, concerning the proponents of alternative methods, that "they often also comment that they are not advocating changes in adjudication (...) building in complementary resolution methods, not usurping current adjudicatory procedures (...) At other points, ADR proponents claim not that ADR is supplementary to but that it mirrors adjudication (...) Two descriptions of ADR and adjudication can therefore be identified, both assuming compatibility but for different reasons. Under one vision, ADR and adjudication are distinct and complementary; one supplements the other. Under the other, the two forms are more similar than distinct. ADR is sufficiently close to adjudication that the two are compatible." Resnik (1995), pp. 253–254.

[16] Identifying this dialogical relationship in English law, Neil Andrews notes that "costs and expense are in the forefront of most people's minds whenever litigation becomes even a remote prospect. Certainly in England, the rise of mediation, notably in high value disputes, is largely attributable to the sheer expense of traditional court litigation. Bill Gates himself, and other modern-day descendants of Croesus, would hesitate to run the risk of engaging in protracted and complicated claims heard by the High Court. The 'Woolf reforms' of 1999 were expected to alleviate the problem of the high cost of civil litigation. But the situation has not improved. And it has been officially recognised that the new procedural code (the CPR 1998) has not reduced the expense of litigation." Andrews (2012), p. 194.

[17] As recognized by Posner, "an economist would consider it natural that a surge in federal caseloads should have led the judiciary and the legal profession to seek to encourage substitute methods of dispute resolution for full-scale federal litigation. The surge increased the (nonmonetary) cost of full-scale federal litigation, and when the cost of a product or service rises, substitutes become more attractive. One substitute for federal judicial services is arbitration, so it is not surprising that the federal courts have become increasingly hospitable to arbitration." Oscar G. Chase also draws this kind of connection between the *crisis* of confidence in state responses and the rise of alternative methods, though from a more philosophical (and less economic) perspective. See Posner (1999), p. 237; Chase (2014), pp. 257–258.

[18] The issue is explained in the work of Cooter and Ulen, emphasizing that "most disputes are resolved without resorting to trial (...) bargaining is more important than trials for the resolution of most disputes. However, bargaining occurs *in the shadow of the law*. In other words, expectations about trials determine the outcomes of bargains (...) in a civil dispute, an agreement to settle out of court can replicate any judgment that the court would have reached after a trial (...) thus, a settlement could achieve the same outcome as a trial, and the parties would save the costs of litigation. The savings in the cost of a trial could have been divided between the parties, making both of them better off. For any trial, a settlement usually exists that makes both parties better off, so trials are usually inefficient." Cooter and Ulen (2000), pp. 398–399.

[19] As observed by Galanter, "for a long time, the great majority of cases of almost every kind in both federal and state courts have terminated by settlement. This reflects the exigencies of litigation, which lead parties to trade off the possibility of preferred outcomes for avoidance of the costs and risks of proceeding through trial. It also reflects the architecture of the system, which has capacity to give full treatment to only a minority of the matters entitled to invoke it. Instead, it

Nevertheless, this interpretation seems to overlook an essential point for the more appropriate use of alternative dispute resolution methods. Generally speaking, these mechanisms are not indiscriminately suitable for any type of dispute. On the one hand, it must be acknowledged that the circumstances of each case mean that the possibility of reaching an agreement is not always readily available. On the other hand, since arbitration is characterized by its ability to address complex and specific disputes, this should be the appropriate field for its application. Otherwise, its very core element, related to the quality of the decision, could be compromised.

- Dispute resolution mechanisms such as arbitration, mediation, and conciliation should ideally be regarded as appropriate responses for disputes that are compatible with their specific characteristics. This is their primary function and main contribution to the justice system, rather than merely serving as an alternative to the judiciary.

Thus, we believe it is illusory to conceive of these dispute resolution mechanisms as a true substitute for state activity. In the words of Mancuso, "*apparently (...) the worse the performance of the state justice system, the more the number, variety, and credibility of jurisdictional equivalents would grow. This 'the worse, the better' logic, however, should neither be sought nor encouraged, because, in the end, it will lead to a zero-sum game in which everyone loses.*"[20] This seems to us to be the central conclusion, demonstrating that while the appreciation of these means is warranted, it does not serve as a solution for everything.

---

relies on a combination of cost barriers (not only out-of-pocket expenditures, but queues and risk) to induce parties to abandon claims or negotiate a settlement on the basis of the signals and markers that it generates." Galanter (2004), pp. 515–516.

[20] In this scenario, the author states that "the state justice system will remain deficient in quality and productivity, and the para-state forums will not be able to absorb the influx of litigants disappointed with the Judiciary. Indeed, *alternative dispute resolution mechanisms*, since they are not funded by the State, experience limited growth and cannot keep pace *pari passu* with the increasing demand for swift, informal, and low-cost justice. On the other hand, the limited efficiency of the state justice system must be addressed by *all available means* (…). Therefore, both the disparaging (and discriminatory) attitude towards alternative mechanisms and the defeatist stance towards the state justice system are unsustainable." In the same vein, Galanter and Lande emphasize that "in a world in which the governmental machinery for redressing injustice does not have the capacity to handle all of its potential business, it is good that government is not the only producer of justice. But government is not only the largest single producer of justice, it also regulates the trade in justice services, directly (by prescribing some procedures of private courts) and indirectly (by establishing public norms influencing private courts and by selectively enforcing decisions) (…) Attention to private alternatives should not be an excuse to permit public courts to decay. We believe that public courts will continue to play the preeminent role in the administration of justice and accordingly deserve undiminished support." Along the same lines, Hensler notes that "ADR practitioners – particularly mediators – have long emphasized the qualitative benefits of substituting problem-solving processes for adjudication. But it is indisputable that ADR has been 'sold' within the court context as a set of procedures for reducing judicial caseloads and cutting time to disposition. ADR proponents have therefore been disappointed by research suggesting that cost and time savings may be illusory." See Mancuso (2014), pp. 273–274. Galanter and Lande (1992). Hensler (1999), p. 15.

On the other hand, we consider that in the continental legal system, the use of alternative dispute resolution methods has often encountered obstacles that prevent them from fulfilling their intended purpose. In summary, while mechanisms such as conciliation or arbitration could play an important role in dispute resolution, we believe that their optimal use requires a cultural shift.[21] To truly value these mechanisms, it is necessary to acknowledge that traditional jurisdiction alone is no longer sufficient.

As can be seen, this observation engages with various pillars discussed throughout the work. From the insufficiency of the state model to the impossibility of absolute interpretations of procedural concepts, there are several factors that discourage an overly generous reading of access to the Courts.[22] Thus, these parallel avenues could play an effective role within the social framework, complementing (rather than excluding) judicial activity.

However, reflecting the very disconnect between legal texts and reality, it is common for civil procedure to overlook this aspect. As a result, the Judiciary is conceived as having its doors open without restriction to any case. This leads to missed opportunities for the development of procedural law, which would benefit from a more realistic assessment of the issue.

6.2 Collective Proceedings and Procedural Management

To a large extent, the reservations raised in the previous section highlight the insufficiency of the traditional discourse on access to justice. In light of these considerations, we argue that it is no longer feasible to treat this guarantee as entirely synonymous with access to the courts. Moreover, in this section, we intend to

[21] As Auerbach states, in a conclusion fully applicable to our reality, "it is a fantasy to believe that mediation or arbitration can now achieve what the law has not accomplished. The deification by Americans of individual rights requires a legal system accessible for their protection. It is understandable that disbelief in the capabilities of this system leads to a longing for alternatives. But the rhetoric of 'community' and 'justice' should not be allowed to conceal the deterioration of community life and the deconstruction of substantive notions of justice that have accompanied its demise. There are numerous reasons why the values historically associated with informal justice remain attractive: chiefly the preference for trust, harmony, and reciprocity in a community context. However, these are not the values that American society encourages or sustains; in their absence, there is no effective alternative to legal institutions." Auerbach (2007), p. 60.

[22] In Mancuso's words, "the *demand-driven* or *judicialist* culture has increasingly taken root in Brazilian society, largely due to an exaggerated, perhaps naïve and unrealistic, interpretation of the guarantee of access to justice (Federal Constitution, art. 5, XXXV), so that the Judiciary has become the general and indiscriminate outlet for any and all resisted or unsatisfied claims, even encompassing disputes that verge on mere whim or a spirit of emulation, including controversies of minimal pecuniary value or no legal complexity whatsoever. Such cases, in truth, do not justify judicialization, in line with the wise Roman maxim – *de minimis non curat praetor* – and can and should be resolved by other means, before other bodies, outside and beyond the state judicial apparatus." Mancuso (2014), p. 108.

demonstrate that even within the judicial sphere, it is necessary to reconsider this concept, making room for new approaches.

Delving deeper into this issue, it is important to recall that over the past decades, civil procedure has embraced the concept of "access to justice" as a central tenet, assigning significant importance to this notion. Nevertheless, it is also appropriate here to raise some questions: what exactly is this "right of access"? What are its content and scope?

In line with the perspective presented throughout this work, we consider that these responses are relative and cultural; they are contextual aspects, as observed by Cappelletti and Garth.[23] Thus, in a framework essentially shaped by liberal values, "access to justice" was also interpreted within these boundaries. On the other hand, with the imposition of new parameters for dispute resolution, the interpretation of the concept was also modified—acquiring greater substantive depth.[24]

However, at this juncture, civil procedure is currently experiencing a moment of inflection. Even though its theory has acquired sophisticated features and its promises have become broader, it is necessary to bring this discourse closer to its real possibilities. The concept of "access to justice" should also be subject to this assessment: seeking to bridge the gap between theory and practice, it would be necessary to rethink its techniques in order to realize this guarantee in a proportional manner.[25]

---

[23] Indeed, analyzing the content attributed to the guarantee, the authors establish as a premise that "the concept of access to justice has undergone a significant transformation, corresponding to an equivalent change in the study and teaching of civil procedure. In liberal 'bourgeois' states (...) it essentially meant the individual's *formal* right, if aggrieved, to bring or contest a lawsuit (...) legal scholars, like the judiciary itself, were removed from the real concerns of the majority of the population." From this, they clarify that "as laissez-faire societies grew in size and complexity (...) it is not surprising (...) that the right to effective access to justice has received particular attention (...) In fact, the right to effective access has been progressively recognized as being of paramount importance among the new individual and social rights, since the mere possession of rights is meaningless in the absence of mechanisms for their effective enforcement. Access to justice can, therefore, be regarded as the fundamental requirement—the most basic of human rights—of a modern and egalitarian legal system that seeks to guarantee, and not merely proclaim, the rights of all (...) its study presupposes a broadening and deepening of the objectives and methods of modern legal science." See Cappelletti and Garth (1988), pp. 09–12.

[24] In this regard, Ada Pellegrini Grinover pointed out nearly three decades ago that "access to justice is not to be confused with, nor is it exhausted by, the mere possibility for everyone to bring their claims before the courts; rather, it means the opportunity for effective and concrete judicial protection, through due process, understood as a set of guarantees that truly enables the parties to present their arguments, produce their evidence, and influence the judge's decision-making process." Grinover (1987), p. 69.

[25] Observing this gap between theory and practice in American law—a criticism that can certainly be extended to the Brazilian model—Rhode states that "'equal justice' is one of America's most proudly proclaimed and widely violated legal principles. It embellishes courthouse entrances, ceremonial occasions, and constitutional decisions. But it comes nowhere close to describing the legal system in practice. Millions of Americans lack any access to justice, let alone equal access (...) we tolerate a system in which money often matters more than merit, and equal protection principles are routinely subverted in practice. This is not, of course, the only legal context in which rhetoric outruns reality. But it is one of the most disturbing, given the fundamental right at issue." Rhode (2004), p. 03.

Among the alternatives aimed at this purpose, we believe that the collective protection of individual rights through a single action could play an important role. The issue, previously discussed in greater detail elsewhere,[26] can be briefly described as follows: given the similarity of certain individual interests, it would be feasible to protect them jointly through a single action. Under our legal system, these would be considered "homogeneous individual rights," allowing for both the filing of numerous individual actions and their consolidation into a single lawsuit.

- To provide greater clarity on this point, it is useful to once again resort to an example. For this purpose, let us imagine that during the first four months of 2021, bank Y deducts fixed amounts from each of its account holders, justifying it as a possible "maintenance fee." Likewise, let us suppose that among these account holders are A, B, and C.

In this context, it is clear that any of the three consumers could bring their individual claim before the court, challenging the legality of the charge and seeking reimbursement of the amounts paid.

However, even in this initial scenario, this individualistic structure of debate would entail a latent risk. This is because, if A, B, and C were to pursue their interests separately before the Judiciary, there would be no guarantee that the same judge would be responsible for analyzing all the cases. As a result, there would be no assurance that the same response would be given to each party, creating the possibility that individuals (despite being in identical legal situations) might receive different treatment from the judicial body.

This scenario would become even more problematic when we consider that, in the case under analysis, it is quite plausible that the matter would not be brought to court solely by A, B, and C, but rather by a multitude of consumers. As a result, the risk of a breach of equality and unpredictability becomes almost certain: with thousands of lawsuits concerning the same charge, it is unrealistic to assume that each would be treated in exactly the same manner. Thus, the very unity of the legal system would be put at risk.[27]

As can be seen, this situation would create a blind spot in the proceedings. In summary, the fragmentation of similar issues would generate a constant risk that analogous situations would be addressed inconsistently. It is precisely in the face of

---

[26] See Osna (2014).

[27] "It is common for one of our federal judges to order the Union to provide a certain medication in a given week, while in the office next door, the doctrine of the 'reserve of the possible' is used to justify the rejection of an identical claim. It is also not unusual for some candidates in a public examination to obtain, through judicial means, the annulment of a question for which the answer key was unfavorable to them (thus benefiting from the corresponding score), while others do not. In such cases, where the situation is the same, the existence of conflicting decisions undermines isonomy and substantive equality (…) analysis of the problem confirms that the technique of collectivization is one of the tools suitable for its resolution. Indeed, by grouping related rights in a single proceeding, it is ensured that all will be protected by a single judgment, thus preventing the conflicts inherent to fragmentation." Osna (2014), pp. 104–105. See also Mendes (2009), pp. 35–36.

such a dilemma that the aggregation of interests would come into play: even though the rights would retain their individual nature, another procedural avenue would be made available to them—allowing a single measure to encompass the claims of all account holders.[28]

From this initial perspective, it is already evident that the aggregation of individual interests could represent an important avenue for procedural law. Moreover, there are additional factors that would further encourage the use of this technique, demonstrating its potential benefits for a reconstruction of the discipline that is more closely aligned with its real possibilities.

Presenting these topics schematically, we can immediately highlight a second benefit brought by this possibility. In cases such as the one described above, it would be quite reasonable to assume that the performance of traditional proceedings would be inadequate for both parties: even if the illegality of the charge were predominantly recognized, there would be various consumers who would tend not to pursue their individual claims (either due to discouragement or inability). On the other hand, even if the legality of the fee were predominantly decided, the financial institution would likely continue to face various lawsuits related to the issue without achieving any real resolution.

Regarding the first of these points, although any of the aggrieved parties could individually seek redress, it is likely that some of them would never become aware of the irregularity.[29] Furthermore, even among those who possessed such information, there would likely be individuals who either lacked appropriate mechanisms to bring a claim to court or were insufficiently motivated to do so—given the transac-

---

[28] As Arenhart states, "the technique of collectivizing the handling of individual issues is, strictly speaking, simply a way to rationalize the provision of judicial services, without any kind of violation of the parties' guarantees." Along the same lines, Teori Zavascki emphasizes that "homogeneous individual rights are, quite simply, individual subjective rights. The qualification of 'homogeneous' does not alter nor can it distort their nature. It is a term used to identify a set of individual subjective rights connected by a relationship of affinity, similarity, or homogeneity, which allows for their collective protection (…) Homogeneous individual rights are, in fact, those same common or related rights addressed in Article 46 of the Code of Civil Procedure (notably in items II and IV), whose collectivization has a merely instrumental purpose, as a strategy to enable their more effective judicial protection." Likewise, Teresa Wambier highlights that "the scenario of a class action seeking protection for homogeneous individual rights consists of the 'collectivized' procedural treatment given to substantially identical claims, which would not justify (although this is, of course, possible) individualized treatment, under penalty of violating the principle of procedural economy and creating the undesirable risk of different decisions for identical situations or cases." See Arenhart (2013), p. 186; Zavascki (2014), pp. 34–35; Alvim (2006), p. 266.

[29] This refers to what Cappelletti and Garth call "personal legal capacity," referring to the "numerous barriers that must be *personally* overcome before a right can actually be asserted through our judicial system." To clarify, they state that "at the first level is the issue of recognizing the existence of a legally enforceable right. This fundamental barrier is especially serious for the dispossessed, but it does not affect only the poor. It concerns the entire population in many types of disputes involving rights (…) even well-informed consumers, for example, rarely realize that their signature on a contract does not necessarily mean they must submit to its terms under all circumstances. They lack the basic legal knowledge not only to object to such contracts, but even to perceive that they may be subject to objection." Cappelletti and Garth (1988), pp. 22–23.

tion costs inherent to the legal process. In any of these scenarios, a bottleneck in our judicial structure would be evident, resulting in a dual risk: denying protection to the interests at stake and allowing the collective defendant to benefit from its wrongful conduct.

This type of risk would become even more pronounced in situations where the harm, viewed from a purely individual perspective, is minimal. This is what American legal doctrine refers to as a *small claim*;[30] that is, interests that, under a "slow analysis," would never reach the courts or receive state protection.[31] The disincentive to individual action would be evident, highlighting a failure of state activity and making unlawful conduct an attractive option. In this context, by imparting a collective dimension to the issue, collective action mechanisms could serve as an important remedy.

Similarly, the use of this procedural pathway could also help address the second issue inherent in the relationship between similar claims and case management: the lack of legal certainty for the defendant who is in the right. In summary, the possibility that the same issue could be brought before the court numerous times by different parties would require the defendant to defend themselves on multiple occasions, even after having already demonstrated the lawfulness of their conduct.

In this regard, the central issue appears to be the impossibility of the proceedings being tailored solely to the interests of the plaintiff. As noted by Mulheron, the defendant must also have their legal certainty and stability proportionally safeguarded.[32] The fragmentation of related issues tends to run counter to this principle, resulting in undue and unnecessary liabilities.

---

[30] Regarding small claims and their particular significance in the field of consumer relations, see Gilles (2009).

[31] The expression was coined by Kahneman, who divides the human mind into two systems: the first (System 1) operates instinctively, quickly, and almost automatically, giving prominence to subjective intuitions; the second (System 2) relegates these intuitions to the background, functioning in a more calculated and rational manner. Kahneman emphasizes that, on numerous occasions, we fail to properly engage System 2 because we overvalue the potential of our intuitions, thereby making mistakes that could be avoided through the "slow" analysis enabled by the use of the "rational system." See Kahneman (2011).

[32] "The second caveat is that access to justice is 'a two-way street': class action jurisprudence must also seek to ensure that the defendant is protected from unmeritorious claims, and understands, and can plead a defense to, the case brought against it. Class action statutes are intended to set up a procedural mechanism only, not to create any new cause of action to confront the defendant. Having said that, however, it is judicially acknowledged that procedural statutes by their very nature can have far-reaching effects upon substantive justice, and the class action legislation is no exception. Moreover, the use of the class action device to protect the defendant from inconsistent obligations that may be created by varying results in different courts has already been noted. In addition, 'defendants should not have to spend money or face adverse publicity as a result of unfounded claims brought against them'—'the procedural balance must not be tipped too far on the side of the plaintiffs.' For whatever the language used in the class action statutes of the focus jurisdictions which may reflect an endorsement of class proceedings, the experience to date has shown that there remains considerable scope for the defendant to attack successfully their commencement on legal, procedural, financial and factual grounds." Mulheron (2004), p. 57.

After all, what is the monthly cost for a company to manage mass litigation? Is this loss ultimately passed on to the consumer market?

Although proceduralists do not yet seem to have given much attention to this aspect, we believe that an analysis such as the one proposed here should take it into account. This is a consequence of the attempt to connect theory with reality, thereby creating a more favorable environment for the effectiveness of the discipline.

Finally, there is yet another aspect that appears to us as fundamental to the possibility of consolidating individual interests within a single proceeding, directly contributing to the judicial activity. As is logically observed, this approach allows for the optimization of structures related to the discipline. It reduces the number of measures, enabling a more appropriate analysis and understanding.

- To clarify this point, it is worth recalling the example already mentioned in this section, related to financial institution Y and its questionable charge. In that case, it was observed that there is a real risk that many consumers would not bring the matter before the courts. However, what would happen if many did? How would this issue impact the judicial system?

Upon analyzing the issues, we observe that certain situations could trigger a dangerous *tsunami* of lawsuits. In a rather irrational manner, the *same* debate would be fragmented into different proceedings. Although the claim would be identical, thousands of actions would be linked to it, requiring the Judiciary to allocate its resources in a disproportionately unreasonable way.[33] This would thus compromise its functioning, given the prodigious increase in demand without a corresponding capacity to respond.[34]

[33] The criticism is forcefully presented by Mancuso, who warns that "the provision of state justice for any and all disputes ultimately produces three harmful effects: it encourages litigiousness within society; discourages the pursuit of alternative means; and, furthermore, results in an overload of the Judiciary, burdening it with cases that could and should have been resolved in other forums." Thus, the author argues that "the millions of cases currently pending in our state judicial system largely stem from an exaggerated and unrealistic interpretation of access to justice." Mancuso (2014), pp. 66–67.

[34] As identified by Posner when describing a similar problem in the U.S. federal sphere, "in a private market, an unexpected rise in demand has two effects, provided the producers are operating at their full capacity. In the short run, when (by definition) producers are unable to expand their productive capacity, price rises to ration demand to the existing fixed supply. In the long run, when producers can expand their capacity, supply increases to accommodate as much as possible of the higher demand, and price falls, though rarely to its level before demand rose. The response of the federal judiciary to the steep and unexpected rise in the demand for its services that began around 1960 has not followed this pattern." Furthermore, due to the political burden that increasing the cost of access to the courts could entail, the author notes that "without ever clearly acknowledging their policy, the people who control the federal court system (members of Congress, executive branch officials, judges, and judicial administrators) have acted consistently as if they had an unshakable commitment to accommodating any increase in the demand for federal judicial services without raising the price of those services, directly (as by filing fees) or indirectly (as by imposing delay), in the short run or the long run, with the partial exception of the increased minimum amount in controversy in diversity cases (…) the political appeal of this response is evident." See Posner (1999), pp. 124–128.

As a result, consolidating this series of interests into a single claim would constitute a beneficial measure for judicial management in such cases.[35] If a thousand disputes could correspond to a thousand unprotected interests, or to a thousand separate proceedings, this technique allows all of them to be safeguarded through a single action.[36]

In this way, the procedural option would be grounded in the principles discussed throughout this work. Generally speaking, the aim is to render the judicial process more proportionate, adapting it to the possibilities and needs of our current social environment.[37] Along these lines, there is room for the reconstruction of its concepts

---

[35] In summary, as we have stated on another occasion, "by consolidating individual rights, claims that would otherwise be adjudicated numerous times by multiple judges can be resolved in a single proceeding, undergoing only one evidentiary phase and resulting in a single decision. This leads to savings in both human and material resources, allowing the judge to devote more time to the dispute and preventing several judges from having to rule successively on related cases. From this perspective, collectivization is a measure to optimize the exercise of jurisdiction and the judicial process; it is a matter of case management (…) in this regard, the technique aligns with important interpretive guidelines highlighted at the outset of this work (such as judicial management) and recognizes that the adaptation of contemporary procedure to its practical realities does not depend solely on strictly legal issues." Osna (2014), p. 101. In this sense, Gidi emphasizes that "the most immediate goal of collective actions is to provide procedural efficiency and economy, by allowing a multitude of repetitive individual actions concerning the same dispute to be replaced by a single collective action (…) the possibility of adjudicating a complex controversy involving numerous individuals in a single proceeding, on the other hand, represents a remarkable saving for the Judiciary." Along the same lines, Laughlin states that "historically, the class action was developed as a mechanism to vindicate in one suit the claims of a group of individuals with common grievances. Three fundamental policy considerations underlie the class action concept: reducing the burden on the courts; eliminating the risk to parties of inconsistent determinations by different courts relating to the same issue; and most importantly, providing a vehicle for redressing small injuries to a large number of persons." Gidi (2007), p. 26. Laughlin (1976), p. 101. See also Arenhart (2013), pp. 152–153.

[36] "By adjudicating lots of otherwise separate suits in one proceeding, the class action avoids the high social costs of relitigating issues common to the different suits (…) there is considerable benefit in being able to litigate the common issues only once, and that benefit increases with the size of the class and the number of common issues." Bone (2003), p. 262.

[37] As noted by Ragone, this judgment of conformity is a true and necessary consequence of the inclusion within the framework of values endowed with greater social assertion. In his words, "the new demands for justice in the social and economic spheres required greater and easier access to the courts, coupled with the need for a prompt response. At the time, this was considered by many to be a basic good of life, especially for the less affluent classes. One must recall the influence of Anton Menger on Klein, whose vision of the joint work of the State with its citizens was based on the need for a collective project for the common good. This ultimately translated into the need for a civil justice system that was open and accessible to all citizens, not only for claims related to property rights and of high value, but also for the social and economic claims of the less privileged classes. This facilitated access to legal advice and to justice, the establishment of mechanisms to allow litigation in some cases without costs or expenses, and the expansion and improvement of legal and juridical assistance by the State to ensure equality of arms and access to the courts. This was the basis for arguing that there was no reason not to accommodate within the judicial system the conflicts arising from industrialization and mass production, and that, therefore, it was no longer sufficient to have proceedings without the State's active involvement to achieve a better, less costly, and more effective judicial outcome." Ragone (2014), p. 249.

and guarantees, moving away from absolute interpretations and recognizing the need for their reconfiguration.

Furthermore, it is important to emphasize that this attempt to reconstruct procedural institutions is also grounded in concrete reality. From a regulatory perspective, different jurisdictions have sought to establish mechanisms aimed at the collectivization of individual interests, pursuing some of the benefits already described in this section.

- The most emblematic paradigm of this aspect is provided by the United States class actions, established in that legal system by Federal Rule 23.[38] Despite the various criticisms directed at it,[39] this mechanism has enjoyed decades of academic and practical prominence in the American context.[40] It is a successful case of critical reconstruction of procedural law.

Summarizing its procedure, we can state that the US class action begins with the filing of an originally individual lawsuit within which collective certification is requested. This conversion is subject to the fulfillment of both general requirements set forth in Rule 23(a)[41] and specific prerequisites set forth in Rule 23(b).[42] Depending on the latter, the procedure may take on different characteristics,

[38] On this subject, in Brazilian legal scholarship, see, for example, Gidi (2007), Roque (2013), and Tucci (1990).

[39] See Redish (2009). Also, for a critical perspective on various aspects related to the application of the U.S. class action, see Nagareda (2007).

[40] On the development of the mechanism, see Hensler (2000), pp. 10–11.

[41] "(a) Prerequisites. One or more members of a class may sue or be sued as representative parties on behalf of all members only if: (1) the class is so numerous that joinder of all members is impracticable; (2) there are questions of law or fact common to the class; (3) the claims or defenses of the representative parties are typical of the claims or defenses of the class; and (4) the representative parties will fairly and adequately protect the interests of the class."

[42] "(b) A class action may be maintained if Rule 23(a) is satisfied and if: (1) prosecuting separate actions by or against individual class members would create a risk of: (A) inconsistent or varying adjudications with respect to individual class members that would establish incompatible standards of conduct for the party opposing the class; or (B) adjudications with respect to individual class members that, as a practical matter, would be dispositive of the interests of the other members not parties to the individual adjudications or would substantially impair or impede their ability to protect their interests; (2) the party opposing the class has acted or refused to act on grounds that apply generally to the class, so that final injunctive relief or corresponding declaratory relief is appropriate respecting the class as a whole; or (3) the court finds that the questions of law or fact common to class members predominate over any questions affecting only individual members, and that a class action is superior to other available methods for fairly and efficiently adjudicating the controversy. The matters pertinent to these findings include: (A) the class members' interests in individually controlling the prosecution or defense of separate actions; (B) the extent and nature of any litigation concerning the controversy already begun by or against class members; (C) the desirability or undesirability of concentrating the litigation of the claims in the particular forum; and (D) the likely difficulties in managing a class action."

assigning varying content to issues such as the possibility of individual withdrawal from the action (opt-out).[43]

Alongside this technique, and although not reaching the same level of effectiveness, the Brazilian legal system also sought to engage in this context—establishing a model of collective action for the protection of individual rights. With this aim, through a symbiotic reading of the Consumer Protection Code and the Public Civil Action Law, the concept of "homogeneous individual rights" was created, and a legal action was devised to provide for their collective protection.[44]

In any case, analysis of the tool demonstrates that there are various problematic aspects related to the very attempt to combine procedural innovation with the classical dogmas of procedure.[45] In our view, this approach seems doomed to failure, as it is not possible to give effect to aggregation without reconstructing the traditional discourse on the subject. The premises established throughout this work seem to facilitate this path and may contribute to our current system of dispute resolution.

6.3 Compositional Process: Structural Decisions and Social Impact

In the previous sections, we highlighted some of the opportunities that a more critical analysis of civil procedure can offer. At this point, we seek to add a final piece to this puzzle: increasingly, the discipline has come to play a significant role in

[43] "As the name would imply, the Rule 23(a) prerequisites for class certification are just that: prerequisites. Rule 23(b) then requires that a court finding that the prerequisites are met determine which of the three primary sorts of class action is to be created. The distinct class action types correspond to familiar problems in the joinder rules, responding to competing demands for insufficient resources, the indivisibility of the remedies sought by the class, or the simple efficiency commands of aggregate treatment of small claims that would not merit prosecution on their own." Issacharoff (2005), p. 79.

[44] See Osna (2014).

[45] "An analysis of our microsystem reveals that the central obstacle to collectivization in Brazilian law is not merely normative. On the contrary, we identify at its core two cultural factors that predate legislation and are responsible for shaping its content: liberal individualist thought and the consequent belief that legal proceedings cannot affect an individual without their expression of will (…) Underlying this is the attempt to preserve individual material interests and individual procedural guarantees intact, preventing an individual from being harmed or even directly benefited by collective action without having taken any initiative. As can be seen, the concern is exactly the same as that which we previously identified as responsible for the development of the substantive view of 'homogeneous individual rights' as an autonomous category of interest. The aim is to reconcile the technique of collectivization with liberal civil procedure. However, this creates a clear obstacle to the functionality of the instrument (…) this is the central issue: subjecting an individual who did not personally participate in the proceedings to the finality and applicability of its decision." In light of this, "it follows (…) that the effectiveness of aggregation will be directly related to the way it is shaped in view of the individual values of the judicial process, and this is the determining aspect of its procedural construction. If primacy is given to the liberal mindset, it is unlikely that the collective protection of rights will adequately achieve any of its purposes. However, if collectivization is prioritized, it is also necessary to accept the structural reinterpretations it entails." Osna (2014), pp. 133–138.

shaping the social order. It has assumed prospective functions, with horizons that extend beyond its traditional language.

- In summary, over the past few years, various countries have experienced an increased judicialization of life. In this context, the judiciary has not only faced a numerical rise in cases but also the challenge of addressing more complex and impactful issues. As a result, it has assumed a regulatory role—requiring a reassessment of its techniques and encouraging the development of new mechanisms such as structural decisions.

To clarify this issue, it is worth recalling once again the example presented in the previous section. There, we hypothesized the existence of a financial institution ("Y") that made questionable charges to all its account holders. In that context, we also mentioned the possibility that the amounts charged, when considered individually, might be minimal. Finally, we reaffirmed that one possible approach would be to aggregate the series of interests in a single legal action.

Against this backdrop, several considerations may arise. How can the limited nature of individual interests be reconciled with the global impact brought about by the situation? In what way can these aspects be connected, allowing the issue to be perceived both in its limited scope and in its broader context?

The relevance of these questions has led some theorists to identify here the main benefit of the very collectivization of interests. By imparting a general character to the issue, this technique would prevent the perpetuation of a globally harmful scenario.[46] Furthermore, it would have a prospective aspect, serving as a form of deterrence.[47]

---

[46] Analyzing *class actions*, and especially those involving small claims, Gilles and Friedman argue that this broad impact would be the main benefit of the mechanism, attributing to it a deterrent role. In their words, "the primary goal in small-claims class actions is deterrence, and that the only question we should ask with respect to any rule or reform proposal in this area is whether it promotes or optimizes deterrence. Once we abandon our obsession with agency costs and windfall fees, discard our compensationalist lenses, and pledge fealty to the one true value of compelling corporate defendants to internalize the social costs of their actions, everything takes on a new light. An examination of some of the hot-button issues in the class action arena bears this out." Also from this macro perspective, Richard Posner conceives collective redress as a mechanism primarily aimed at the redistribution of resources, the purpose of which is to prevent the serial defendant from benefiting from their wrongdoing. Thus, "the most important point, on an economic analysis, is that the violator be confronted with the costs of his violation – this achieve the allocative purpose of the suit – not that he pay them to his victim." Gilles and Friedman (2006), p. 139. Posner (1977), pp. 449–450.

[47] "Class actions can serve an important role in deterrence as a useful complement to the underfunded and overburdened public enforcement system (…) ex-post private regulation through aggregate litigation is an important complement to market liberalization (…) what sets the United States apart is the fact that its basic regulatory model is ex-post rather than ex-ante (…) the American tendency to litigate about topics that are handled without litigation in other societies is not pathological, but rather a logical consequence of the American method of providing activist government without a centralized bureaucracy." Issacharoff (2012), pp. 39–41.

Broadening our perspective, we observe that the inclusion of civil procedure within this more extensive and complex dimension becomes even more evident due to the fact that essentially collective interests have also entered the scope of the discipline, including positions of a supra-individual nature.[48] Their recognition redefines the role of our judicial structure, imparting new characteristics to its framework.[49]

Indeed, it was identified that the discipline was shaped by liberal values such as individualism and the strict separation between the public and private spheres. As observed, these guidelines were appropriate for a movement toward the centralization of power, demonstrating contextual suitability.

In this context, dispute resolution would invariably be conceived to address two very specific interests: to settle a conflict between "A" and "B." Its subjective dimension would be limited, involving two clearly defined parties. In its lexicon, there would be no room for other expressions.

It should be noted, however, as observed throughout the study, that this ideological framework has not remained unscathed over the past century. The cultural changes experienced have introduced new spheres of demand. There has been a restructuring, leading to the realization that, in addition to the individual and the State, there are also collectives. The legal sphere, with its cultural background, has not remained indifferent to this development.

Indeed, social changes have compelled legal scholars to adapt, recognizing that there are positions whose ownership cannot be individually expressed or reduced.[50] These interests would belong to groups, and their protection would not benefit a single individual, but rather meta-individual aspirations. Ultimately, these are essentially collective rights.

- This shift can be observed in the increased emphasis on environmental protection. Although the assets comprising this interest have historically existed, their recognition by the law is more recent. The situation itself is not new; it is now receiving greater attention.

---

[48] "Collective rights are subjectively *transindividual* rights (= without a specific holder) and materially *indivisible*. Collective rights can be understood in the singular, including for the purposes of judicial protection. In other words: although indivisible, it is possible to conceive of a single unit of the category of collective right (…) This term is used to designate a special category of substantive right, which emerged from the now undisputed overcoming of the traditional dichotomy between public and private interest. It is a right that belongs neither to the public administration nor to specifically determined individuals. Rather, it belongs to a group of people, a class, a category, or to society itself, considered in its broadest sense." Zavascki (2014), pp. 33–34. See also Arenhart (2013).

[49] See, among others, Ribeiro (2010). Also, for an analysis of transindividual interests from a historical perspective, see Mancuso (2013), p. 42. Additionally, on this topic, see Venturi (2007), p. 50.

[50] "Endowed with a very high degree of humanism and universality, third-generation rights tend to crystallize at the end of the twentieth century as rights that are not specifically intended to protect the interests of an individual, a group, or a particular State. Their primary addressee is humanity itself, at a significant moment of its affirmation as the supreme value in terms of concrete existence." Bonavides (2010), p. 569.

In other words, the environment has always existed. Similarly, it is traditionally recognized that the owner of a property also holds ownership of the trees located within its boundaries. What has changed is the perception of this scenario: alongside this preliminary aspect, it has come to be understood that it is necessary to apply another layer of scrutiny to these assets, one of a collective nature.

After all, if trees are understood solely from an individual perspective, would it be possible for each owner to choose to cut them down? If the collective will were to move in that direction, what impact would this have on the community? How can their survival be ensured?

As can be seen, when we view the legal sphere from a purely subjective perspective, there is a serious risk of imbalance. On the other hand, by moving beyond the absolute separation between the State and the individual, a supra-individual dimension is rediscovered. In addition to each individual tree, the forest they form and the environment they compose also come into play—requiring ongoing efforts at adaptation.

In a broad analysis, we can state that different legal systems have established equally diverse methods for addressing these collective positions.[51] In this context, we observe a growing expansion of the role to be played by the judiciary. This phenomenon reflects the very reconfiguration of state powers,[52] raising issues such as the possibility of policy implementation by the courts.[53] In any case, this phenomenon requires a necessary caveat: for the legal process to operate within these new dimensions, we must also conceive of a new process. In light of its current challenges, it is necessary to reconstruct the institutions governing this field.

- This issue becomes clearer when we once again turn to an example. Let us suppose that, in a given municipality, a large portion of the population is served by

[51] "In some countries – even in civil law jurisdictions – the problem of group litigation (or, as it is sometimes defined, the problem of judicial protection of collective, diffuse, and supra-individual interests and rights) has been addressed in several ways: new statutory regulations, developments in case law, theoretical debates, and reform projects." Taruffo (2001), p. 405.

[52] Observing this issue, Ackerman states that "Montesquieu did not have the slightest inkling of political parties, democratic politics, modern constitutional designs, contemporary bureaucratic techniques, and the distinctive ambitions of the modern regulatory state. And yet we mindlessly follow him in supposing that all this complexity is best captured by a Trinitarian separation of power into the legislative, judicial and executive (…) almost three centuries later, it is past time to rethink Montesquieu's holy trinity. Despite its canonical status, it is blinding us to the world-wise rise of new institutional form that cannot be neatly categorized as legislative, judicial, or executive (…) a 'new separation of powers' is emerging in the twenty-first century (…) and so we must say a fond farewell to Montesquieu, and create a new foundation for comparative administrative law that is equal to the challenges of modern government." In this regard, Talamini states that "traditionally, there were no major difficulties in distinguishing legislation (the production of innovative general and abstract norms within the legal system) from the other two activities, administration and adjudication, which operate within the scope of applying norms. The greatest difficulties lay in differentiating administration from adjudication. But in the contemporary constitutional framework, the very distinction between legislation and adjudication sometimes risks generating impasses." Ackerman (2010), pp. 128–129. Talamini (2007), p. 232.

[53] On this topic, see Osna (2014), pp. 31–33. See also Arenhart (2005), p. 504.

the same hospital. Imagine, however, that the Public Prosecutor's Office finds that the doctors working at the facility have irregular employment arrangements—bringing the matter before the Judiciary and seeking the immediate dismissal of these professionals.

In this scenario, following a traditional line of reasoning, the judge would simply be tasked with either granting or denying the initial claim, ordering the dismissal of the physicians, or recognizing the legality of their hiring. However, a critical analysis reveals that either outcome would have significant negative consequences: a strict application of the legal text could result in an undesirable burden on public health, while disregarding it would undermine institutional trust itself.

In this context, the only way for procedural intervention to meet actual needs would be to pursue a third path. Although this possibility may seem foreign to the classical framework of the discipline, situations such as this would require some form of ongoing action, subject to successive adaptations.[54] This is what doctrine has referred to as "structural decisions" or "structural proceedings."[55]

Explaining the issue in greater detail, Arenhart accurately points out that "*many decisions regarding collective matters require solutions that go beyond simple rulings on linear relationships between the parties. They demand diffuse responses, with multiple impositions or measures that are implemented gradually*." This is because, in such cases, "*broad societal values come into play, not only in the sense that there are several competing interests at stake, but also because the legal sphere of various third parties may be affected by the judicial decision*."[56] As a result, it would be necessary to restore the judicial process's capacity for action in a manner more attuned to real needs. If the notion of congruence has historically imposed a

[54] It should be noted, moreover, that in a case analogous to the example given, there has already been a judicial ruling to this effect. The issue is explained by Arenhart in the following terms: "It concerned a public civil action filed by the Labor Public Prosecutor's Office, seeking the termination of the contracts of outsourced personnel working at the Hospital de Clínicas of the Federal University of Paraná. According to the Labor Prosecutor's Office, the outsourcing of services (nursing and pharmacy) violated labor regulations, and therefore such contracts should be rescinded. The Federal University of Paraná, however, argued that the immediate termination of these contracts would render the university hospital's activities unfeasible—this hospital is also the main provider of care for the SUS in Paraná—since these workers represented approximately half of the available nursing and pharmacy staff. Clearly, a solution that simply applied labor law and terminated the outsourcing contracts might be formally correct, but would certainly have disastrous consequences for public health management (especially for the poorest populations) in Paraná, as these positions would not be immediately filled by civil servants hired through public examinations. On the other hand, a judgment refusing to terminate such contracts could be seen as incorrect from the perspective of labor law. The solution adopted by the presiding Labor Judge, Dr. Leonardo Wandelli, was to broker a long-term agreement between the parties, establishing targets for the 'replacement' of outsourced workers with public servants. Under the terms of the settlement, the University would dismiss the outsourced workers as it was able to open positions for public recruitment (for the same roles); furthermore, every two years, the parties would meet in court to assess the progress of this 'replacement.' See Arenhart (2013b). See also, Arenhart (2013a).

[55] Idem. See also, on this topic, Violin (2013).

[56] See, for example, Arenhart (2013b).

more limited role on the Judiciary, it would be necessary to redefine it—creating a field in which these structural decisions could play an important role.

Thus, it is argued that judicial decisions must also be subject to a broad logic of proportionality—bringing into question their general effects on the social sphere. In this way, the justice of the individual case is combined with macrojustice, seeking to connect judicial reasoning with the concrete circumstances of society.[57]

Although various criticisms could be directed at this approach, we consider that it also constitutes an important piece in the puzzle of contemporary civil procedure. In short, by introducing new issues into its scope, it becomes necessary to reconfigure its possible responses and modes of operation. It becomes essential to address the discipline with a dynamic perspective, acknowledging its capacity for change.

References

Ackerman, B. (2010). Good-bye, Montesquieu. In S. Rose-Ackerman & P. L. Lindseth (Eds.), *Comparative administrative law*. Edward Elgar.

Alvim, T. A. (2006). Litispendência em ações coletivas. In P. H. S. Lucon (Ed.), *Tutela Coletiva*. Atlas.

Andrews, N. (2012). *The three paths of justice: Courts proceedings, arbitration and mediation in England*. Springer.

Arenhart, S. C. (2005). As ações coletivas e o controle das políticas públicas pelo Poder Judiciário. In R. Mazzei & R. D. Nolasco (Eds.), *Processo civil coletivo*. Quartier Latin.

Arenhart, S. C. (2013a). *A tutela coletiva de interesses individuais: para além da proteção dos interesses individuais homogêneos*. Ed. RT.

Arenhart, S. C. (2013b). Decisões estruturais no direito processual civil brasileiro. *Revista de Processo*, 225.

Auerbach, J. S. (2007). Justiça sem Direito. In A. G. De Azevedo & I. M. Barbosa (Eds.), *Estudos em Arbitragem, Mediação e Negociação*. Universidade de Brasília.

Barrett, J. T., & Barrett, J. P. (2004). *A history of alternative dispute resolution the story of a political, cultural, and social movement*. Jossey-Bass.

Bonavides, P. (2010). *Curso de Direito Constitucional* (25th ed.). Malheiros.

Bone, R. G. (2003). *The economics of civil procedure*. Foundation Press.

Cappelletti, M., & Garth, B. (1988). *Acesso à justiça*. Sérgio Fabris.

Carmona, C. A. (2009). *Arbitragem e Processo*. Atlas.

Chase, O. G. (2014). *Direito, Cultura e Ritual*. Editora Marcial Pons.

Cooter, R., & Ulen, T. (2000). *Law & economics* (3rd ed.). Addison Wesley Longman.

Fiss, O. (2003). *The law as it could be*. New York University Press.

[57] Indeed, it is essential for the judge to weigh the various aspects at stake so that only then can a decision be made in the most appropriate manner, thereby preventing the justice of the case from being transformed into overall injustice. As Richard Posner aptly describes when discussing the American judiciary, "even if judges *wanted* to forswear any legislative, any political, role and be merely the 'oracles' of the law, transmitting directives rather than directing, they could not do so in the condition they found themselves." In this regard, if the objective of the proceedings is to achieve a "structural reform," it is necessary to reinterpret the judicial function as proposed by Owen Fiss, whose perspective indicates that "courts should not be viewed in isolation but as coordinate source of government power," seeking their legitimacy through broad engagement with the community. See Posner (2008), p. 371; Fiss (2003), p. 54.

Fouchard, P., Gaillard, E., & Goldman, B. (1999). *On international commercial arbitration*. Kluwer Law International.

Gabbay, D. M. (2013). *Mediação & Judiciário no Brasil e nos EUA*. Gazeta Jurídica.

Galanter, M. (2004). The vanishing trial: An examination of trials and related matters in federal and state courts. *Journal of Empirical Legal Studies*, 3.

Galanter, M., & Lande, J. (1992). Private courts and public authority. *Studies in Law, Political, Society*, 12.

Gidi, A. (2007). *A class action como instrumento de tutela coletiva de direitos*. Ed. RT.

Gilles, M. (2009). *Class dismissed: Contemporary judicial hostility to small claim consumers class actions* [Cardozo working paper no 278].

Gilles, M., & Friedman, G. B. (2006). Exploding the class action agency costs myth: The social utility of entrepreneurial lawyers. *University of Pennsylvania Law Review*, 155.

Grinover, A. P. (1987). Deformalização do Processo e Deformalização das Controvérsias. *Revista de Processo*, 46.

Hensler, D. R. (1999). A research agenda: What we need to know about court-connected ADR. *Dispute Resolution Magazine*, 15.

Hensler, D. R. (2000). *Class action dilemmas – Pursuing public goals for private gain*. Rand.

Issacharoff, S. (2012). Fairness in aggregation. In E. Oteiza (Ed.), *Processos Colectivos. Class actions*. AADP, IAPL e IIDP.

Issacharoff, S. (2005). *Civil procedure*. Foundation Press.

Kahneman, D. (2011). *Thinking, fast and slow*. Farrar, Straus and Giroux.

Laughlin, J. P. (1976). Federal appellate review of the grant or denial of class action status. *Boston College Industrial and Commercial Law Review*, 18.

Lazari, I., Bolonha, C., & Rangel, H. (2013). A relevância dos limites discricionários do juiz generalista. *Revista Direito GV*, 18.

Lew, J. D., Mistelis, L. A., & Kröll, S. (2003). *Comparative international commercial arbitration*. Kluwers Law International.

Macneil, I. R. (1992). *American arbitration law – Reformation, nationalization, internationalization*. Oxford University Press.

Mancuso, R. C. (2013). *Interesses Difusos* (8 edn. rev.). Ed. RT.

Mancuso, R. C. (2014). *A resolução dos conflitos e a função judicial no contemporâneo Estado de Direito* (2nd ed.). Ed. RT.

Marinoni, L. G., Arenhart, S. C., & Mitidiero, D. (2015a). *Novo Curso de Processo Civil – Tutela dos Direitos Mediante Procedimentos Diferenciados*. Ed. RT.

Marinoni, L. G., Arenhart, S. C., & Mitidiero, D. (2015b). *Novo Curso de Processo Civil – Teoria do Processo Civil*. Ed. RT.

Mendes, A. G. C. (2009). *Ações coletivas no direito comparado e nacional* (2nd ed.). Ed. RT.

Mulheron, R. (2004). *The class action in common law legal systems: A comparative perspective*. Hart Publishing.

Nagareda, R. (2007). *Mass Torts in a world of settlement*. University of Chicago Press.

Osna, G. (2014). *Direitos Individuais Homogêneos: pressupostos, fundamentos e aplicação no processo civil*. Ed. RT.

Posner, R. (1977). *Economic analysis of law* (2nd ed.). Little, Brown and Company.

Posner, R. (1999). *The federal courts – Challenges and reforms*. Harvard University Press.

Posner, R. (2008). *How judges think*. Harvard University Press.

Ragone, A. P. (2014). Retrato del revisionismo garantista en el proceso civil a través de Klein y Wach. *Revista de Processo*, 233.

Redish, M. (2009). *Wholesale justice – Constitutional democracy and the problem of the class action lawsuit*. Stanford University Press.

Resnik, J. (1995). Many doors? Closing doors? Alternative dispute resolution and adjudication. *Ohio State Journal on Dispute Resolution*, 10.

Rhode, D. L. (2004). *Access to justice*. Oxford University Press.

Ribeiro, S. S. M. (2010). *Direitos Coletivos e Liberdade Individual*. Juruá.

Roque, A. V. (2013). *Class action – Ações Coletivas nos Estados Unidos: o que podemos aprender com eles?* Juspodivm.
Talamini, E. (2007). Tutela de Urgência e Fazenda Pública. In C. A. Molinaro, M. G. Milhoranza, & S. G. Porto (Eds.), *Constituição, jurisdição e processo*. Notadez.
Taruffo, M. (2001). Some remarks on group litigation in comparative perspective. *Duke Journal of Comparative & International Law*, 11.
Tucci, J. R. C. (1990). *Class action e mandado de segurança coletivo, diversificações conceptuais*. Ed. RT.
Venturi, E. (2007). *Processo Civil Coletivo*. Malheiros.
Violin, J. (2013). *Protagonismo Judiciário e Processo Coletivo Estrutural*. Editora JusPodivm.
Zavascki, T. A. (2014). *Processo Coletivo – Tutela de direitos coletivos e tutela coletiva de direitos* (6th ed.). Ed. RT.

Chapter 7
Final Considerations

> If a watch is not working, it ought to be fixed. In this example, the 'ought' is derived from two 'is's': that the watch is not working, and that the function of a watch is to tell time.

With the above construction, Richard Posner reminds us that, often, accepting certain statements simplistically can overlook highly relevant underlying elements. This justifies a more skeptical approach, allowing greater room for doubt. Even when faced with the need to repair a clock, it is impossible to disregard a functionalist judgment (assessing whether the repair is, in fact, necessary).

In this work, it is argued that this type of interpretation should also be applied to civil procedural law. Here as well, it is necessary to confront, in a more pragmatic manner, dogmas and certainties that sometimes appear to be "natural."

Does "due process" truly have the scope that is commonly attributed to it in continental legal systems? Can this type of guarantee, along with other principles associated with it (such as the notion of a "day in court"), be interpreted in a manner disconnected from reality?

In the previous chapters, we argued that civil procedure is a cultural construct primarily aimed at legitimization. As a result, it is extremely complex to speak of absolute truths within the discipline. Its requirements are, above all, conjectural.

Considering this aspect, as well as the inherent limitations of its construction, approaching the procedural system proportionally (in the sense attributed throughout the work) appears to be an important solution. Through this approach, the discipline is prevented from being constructed or implemented through a purely theoretical or excessively microscopic perspective. All its actors gain a broad view of the justice system, enabling choices that balance aspects such as its limitations and its possibilities.

This element serves as a gateway to a procedural system that is more attentive to concrete needs than the one typically seen in the continental model. It is recognized that academic perfection is not sufficient. It is essential to strive for the implementation of a fairer and more effective model.

Rather than asserting a definitive approach to the application of procedure, the aim here was to offer a new approach to the very understanding of the subject. This

G. Osna, *Civil Procedure, Culture, and Proportionality*,
https://doi.org/10.1007/978-3-032-27555-4_7

opens up new possibilities, allowing for a more skeptical reading of the material (regarding potential certainties) and a more realistic perspective (regarding possible reforms). A new range of elements must be considered in this articulation, along a path that, in our view, deserves serious consideration.

References

Ackerman, B. (2010). Good-bye, Montesquieu. In S. Rose-Ackerman & P. L. Lindseth (Eds.), *Comparative administrative law*. Edward Elgar Publishing.

Alexy, R. (1993). *Teoria de los derechos fundamentales*. Centro de Estudios Constitucionales.

Allorio, E. (1963). *Problemas de Derecho Procesal*. EJEA.

Alvim, T. A. (2006). Litispendência em ações coletivas. In P. H. S. Lucon (Ed.), *Tutela Coletiva*. Atlas.

Amaral, G. (2001). *Direito, escassez e escolha*. Renovar.

Andrews, N. (2012). *The three paths of justice: Courts proceedings, arbitration and mediation in England*. Springer.

Arenhart, S. C. (2005). As ações coletivas e o controle das políticas públicas pelo Poder Judiciário. In R. Mazzei & R. D. Nolasco (Eds.), *Processo civil coletivo*. Quartier Latin.

Arenhart, S. C. (2013a). *A tutela coletiva de interesses individuais: para além da proteção dos interesses individuais homogêneos*. Ed. RT.

Arenhart, S. C. (2013b). Decisões estruturais no direito processual civil brasileiro. *Revista de Processo*, 225.

Arenhart, S. C., & Osna, G. (2014). Complexity, proportionality and the 'pan-procedural' approach: Some bases of contemporary civil litigation. *International Journal of Procedural Law*, 4.

Auerbach, J. S. (2007). Justiça sem Direito. In A. G. De Azevedo & I. M. Barbosa (Eds.), *Estudos em Arbitragem, Mediação e Negociação*. Universidade de Brasília.

Barcellos, A. P. (2005). *Ponderação, racionalidade e atividade jurisdicional*. Renovar.

Barrett, J. T., & Barrett, J. P. (2004). *A history of alternative dispute resolution the story of a political, cultural, and social movement*. Jossey-Bass.

Barroso, L. R. (2009). *Curso de Direito Constitucional Contemporâneo*. Saraiva.

Becker, H. S. (2007). *Segredos e Truques da Pesquisa*. Zahar.

Becker, L. A. (2012). Erosão do Sagrado Processual. In L. A. Becker (Ed.), *Qual é o jogo do processo?* Sérgio Fabris.

Berger, P. L., & Berger, B. (1977). O que é uma instituição social? In M. M. Foracchi & J. S. Martins (Eds.), *Sociologia e Sociedade: Leitura de introdução à Sociologia*. LTC.

Binenbojm, G. (2006). A constitucionalização do Direito Administrativo: um itinerário de avanços e retrocessos. *Revista Brasileira de Direito Público*, 14.

Bobbio, N. (1995). *O Positivismo Jurídico*. Ícone.

Bobbio, N. (2000). *Igualdade e Liberdade* (4th ed.). Ediouro.

Bonavides, P. (2010). *Curso de Direito Constitucional* (25th ed.). Malheiros.

Bone, R. G. (2003). *The economics of civil procedure*. Foundation Press.

G. Osna, *Civil Procedure, Culture, and Proportionality*, https://doi.org/10.1007/978-3-032-27555-4

Bone, R. G. (2012). Discovery. In C. W. Sanchirico (Ed.), *Procedural law and economics*. Edward Elgar.
Borowski, M. (2003). *La estructura de los derechos fundamentales*. Universidad Externado de Colômbia.
Bourdieu, P. (1989). *O Poder Simbólico*. Difusão Editorial.
Bourdieu, P. (2002). *A Profissão de Sociólogo* (3rd ed.). Editora Vozes.
Bush, R. A., & Folger, J. (2005). *The promise of mediation – The transformative approach to conflict*. John Wiley & Sons.
Cabral, A. P. (2016). *Convenções Processuais*. Juspodivm.
Calabresi, G., & Bobbit, P. (1978). *Tragic choices*. W.W Norton & Company.
Calamandrei, P. (1950). Processo e Giustizia. *Rivista di Diritto Processuale*, 5.
Calamandrei, P. (1956). *Procedure and democracy*. New York University Press.
Calamandrei, P. (1996). *Instituciones de derecho procesal civil* (Vol. 1). El Foro.
Caponi, R. (2011). O princípio da proporcionalidade na justiça civil. *Revista de Processo*, 192.
Cappelletti, M., & Garth, B. (1988). *Acesso à justiça*. Sérgio Fabris.
Carmona, C. A. (2009). *Arbitragem e Processo*. Atlas.
Carnelutti, F. (1958). *Diritto e Processo*. Morano Editore.
Carroll, J. L. (2010). Proportionality in discovery: A cautionary tale. *Campbell Law Review*, 32.
Cavallone, B. (2010). In difesa dela Veriphobia (considerazioni amichevolmente polemiche su un libro recente di Michele Taruffo). *Rivista di Diritto Processuale*, 65.
Chase, O. G. (2014). *Direito, Cultura e Ritual*. Editora Marcial Pons.
Chiarloni, S. (1975). *Introduzione allo studio del diritto processuale*. G. Giappichelli.
Chiovenda, G. (1922). *Principios de Derecho Procesal*. Editorial Réus.
Chiovenda, G. (1993). L'azioni nel sistema dei diritti. In G. Chiovenda (Ed.), *Saggi di Diritto Processuale Civile* (Vol. 1). Giuffrè.
Clermont, K. M. (2005). *Principles of civil procedure*. Thomson West.
Clève, C. M. (1995). A Teoria Constitucional e o Direito Alternativo (por uma dogmática constitucional emancipatória). In C. Lembo (Ed.), *Uma vida dedicada ao Direito – Homenagem a Carlos Henrique de Carvalho*. Ed. RT.
Clève, C. M. (2006). A Eficácia dos Direitos Fundamentais Sociais. *Revista de Direito Constitucional e Internacional*, 54.
Comparato, F. K. (1965). O indispensável direito econômico. *Revista dos Tribunais*, 353.
Cooter, R., & Ulen, T. (2000). *Law & economics* (3rd ed.). Addison Wesley Longman.
Costa, P. (2006). O Estado de Direito: uma introdução histórica. In P. Costa & D. Zolo (Eds.), *O Estado de Direito: história, teoria e crítica*. Martins Fontes.
Coutinho, J. N. M. (1989). *A lide e o conteúdo do processo penal*. Juruá.
Couture, E. J. (1942). *Fundamentos del Derecho Procesal Civil*. Aniceto Lopez Editor.
Cunha, A. (2010). Os desafios ao Estado, à governança e à gestão pública: explorando ideias para subsidiar os esforços de reforma da gestão nas organizações do Poder Judiciário. In J. R. Cunha (Ed.), *Poder Judiciário: Novos Olhares sobre Gestão e Jurisdição*. Editora FGV.
Damaška, M. (1986). *The faces of justice and state authority*. Yale University Press.
Davis, K. E., & Trebilcock, M. J. (2009). A relação entre direito e desenvolvimento: otimistas versus céticos. *Revista Direito GV*, 5.
Denti, V. (1989). *La giustizia civile – Lezioni introduttive*. Il Mulino.
Didier, F., Jr. (2010). *Curso de Direito Processual Civil* (Vol. 1, 12th ed.). Editora JusPodivm.
Dinamarco, C. R. (1987). *A instrumentalidade do processo*. Ed. RT.
Dinamarco, C. R. (2005). *Instituições de Direito Processual Civil* (Vol. 1). Malheiros.
Durkheim, E. (2007). *As regras do método sociológico*. Martins Fontes.
Edwards, T. (2007). *Cultural theory: Classical and contemporary positions*. Sage.
Evans-Pritchard, E. E. (1976). *Withcraft, Oracles, and Magic among the Azande*. Oxford University Press.
Falcão, J. (2004). *Democracia, Direito e Terceiro Setor*. Editora FGV.
Ferraz, T. S., Jr. (2001). *Introdução ao estudo do direito: técnica, dominação e decisão* (3rd ed.). Atlas.

Fiss, O. (1979). The forms of justice. *Harvard Law Review*, 93.
Fiss, O. (1993). The allure of individualism. *Iowa Law Review,* 78.
Fiss, O. (2003). *The law as it could be*. New York University Press.
Fouchard, P., Gaillard, E., & Goldman, B. (1999). *On international commercial arbitration.* Kluwer Law International.
Frank, J. (1949). *Courts on trial*. Princeton University Press.
Frankfurter, H. G. (2015). *On inequality*. Princeton University Press.
Gabbay, D. M. (2013). *Mediação & Judiciário no Brasil e nos EUA*. Gazeta Jurídica.
Galanter, M. (2004). The vanishing trial: An examination of trials and related matters in federal and state courts. *Journal of Empirical Legal Studies,* 3.
Galanter, M., & Lande, J. (1992). Private courts and public authority. *Studies in Law, Political, Society*, 12.
Galdino, F. (2005). *Introdução à Teoria dos Custos dos Direitos – Direitos não nascem em árvores*. Editora Lumen Juris.
Geertz, C. (1973). *The interpretation of cultures*. Basic Books.
Gidi, A. (2007). *A class action como instrumento de tutela coletiva de direitos*. Ed. RT.
Gilles, M. (2009). *Class dismissed: Contemporary judicial hostility to small claim consumers class actions* [Cardozo Working Paper No. 278].
Gilles, M., & Friedman, G. B. (2006). Exploding the class action agency costs myth: The social utility of entrepreneurial lawyers. *University of Pennsylvania Law Review*, 155.
Gilley, B. (2006). The meaning and measure of state legitimacy: Results for 72 countries. *European Journal of Political Research,* 45.
Ginzburg, C. (2001). *Olhos de madeira – novas reflexões sobre a distância*. São Paulo, Companhia das Letras.
Godoy, M. G. (2012). *Constitucionalismo e Democracia – Uma leitura a partir de Carlos Santiago Nino e Roberto Gargarella.* Saraiva.
Gomes, M. E. A. C. (2004). Do Instituto do Ombudsman à construção das ouvidorias públicas no Brasil. In R. P. Lyra (Ed.), *Autônomas x obedientes: a ouvidoria pública em debate.* Editora UFPB.
Gomes, O. (2010). *Direitos Reais* (20th ed.). Forense.
Grinover, A. P. (1987). Deformalização do Processo e Deformalização das Controvérsias. *Revista de Processo*, 46.
Grinover, A. P. (1993). Modernidade do Direito Processual Civil Brasileiro. *Revista da Faculdade de Direito,* 88.
Grossi, P. (2005). *Primeiras lições sobre o Direito*. Forense.
Haack, S. (1996). Concern for truth: What it means, why it matters. In P. R. Gross, N. Levitt, & M. W. Lewis (Eds.), *The flight from science and reason*. New York Academy of Science.
Hart, H. L. A. (1988). *The concept of law*. Oxford University Press.
Hensler, D. R. (1999). A research agenda: What we need to know about court-connected ADR. *Dispute Resolution Magazine*, 15.
Hensler, D. R. (2000). *Class action dilemmas – Pursuing public goals for private gain*. Rand.
Hespanha, A. M. (2005). *Cultura Jurídica Europeia*. Boiteux.
Hespanha, A. M. (2012). *O Caleidoscópio do Direito*. Almedina.
Hodges, C. (2008). *The reform of class and representative actions in European legal systems*. Hart Publishing.
Holmes, S., & Sunstein, C. R. (2000). *The cost of rights – Why liberty depends on taxes*. W.W Norton & Company.
Issacharoff, S. (2005). *Civil procedure*. Foundation Press.
Issacharoff, S. (2012). Fairness in aggregation. In E. Oteiza (Ed.), *Processos Colectivos. Class actions*. AADP, IAPL e IIDP.
Jones, B. D. (1999). Bounded rationality. *Annual Review of Political Science*, 2.
Kahneman, D. (2011). *Thinking, fast and slow*. Farrar, Straus and Giroux.
Keynes, J. M. (1936). *The general theory of employment, interest and money*. Palgrave Macmillan.

Kornhausen, L. (2012). Judicial organization and administration. In C. W. Sanchirico (Ed.), *Procedural law and economics*. Edward Elgar.

Kuttner, R. (1992). *The end of laissez-faire – National purpose and the global economy after the cold war*. University of Pennsylvania Press.

Lacerda, G. (1961). Processo e Cultura. *Revista de Direito Processual Civil*, 3.

Laporte, E. D., & Redgrave, J. M. (2015). A practical guide to achieving proportionality under new federal rule of civil procedure. *The Federal Courts Law Review, 26*, 9.

Laughlin, J. P. (1976). Federal appellate review of the grant or denial of class action status. *Boston College Industrial and Commercial Law Review*, 18.

Lazari, I., Bolonha, C., & Rangel, H. (2013). A relevância dos limites discricionários do juiz generalista. *Revista Direito GV,* 18.

Lew, J. D., Mistelis, L. A., & Kröll, S. (2003). *Comparative international commercial arbitration*. Kluwers Law International.

Liebman, E. T. (1962). L'azione nella teoria del processo civile. In E. T. Liebman (Ed.), *Problemi del Processo Civile*. Morano.

Lindsay, M. J. (2010). In search of 'Laissez-Faire Constitutionalism'. *Harvard Law Review Forum*, 123.

Lyra, R. P. (2011). *Do Tribuno da Plebe ao Ouvidor Público: estudos sobre defensores da cidadania*. João Pessoa.

Macneil, I. R. (1992). *American arbitration law – Reformation, nationalization, internationalization*. Oxford University Press.

Mancuso, R. C. (2011). *Acesso à justiça: condicionantes legítimas e ilegítimas*. Ed. RT.

Mancuso, R. C. (2013). *Interesses Difusos* (8th ed. rev.). Ed. RT.

Mancuso, R. C. (2014). *A resolução dos conflitos e a função judicial no contemporâneo Estado de Direito* (2nd ed.). Ed. RT.

Marinoni, L. G. (2005). *Teoria Geral do Processo*. Ed. RT.

Marinoni, L. G., Arenhart, S. C., & Mitidiero, D. (2015a). *Novo Curso de Processo Civil – Tutela dos Direitos Mediante Procedimentos Diferenciados*. Ed. RT.

Marinoni, L. G., Arenhart, S. C., & Mitidiero, D. (2015b). *Novo Curso de Processo Civil – Teoria do Processo Civil*. Ed. RT.

Marinoni, L. G., Ragone, A. P., & Ojeda, R. N. (2010). *Fundamentos del proceso civil - Hacia una teoría de la adjudicación*. Abeledo Perrot.

Mendes, A. G. C. (2009). *Ações coletivas no direito comparado e nacional* (2nd ed.). Ed. RT.

Miceli, T. J. (2012). The social versus private incentive to sue. In C. W. Sanchirico (Ed.), *Procedural law and economics*. Edward Elgar.

Minkov, M. (2012). *Cross-cultural analysis: The science and art of comparing world's modern societies and their cultures*. Sage.

Miranda, J. (2003). *Manual de Direito Constitucional* (Vol. 1, 7th ed.). Coimbra Editora.

Mitidiero, D. (2004). Processo e Cultura: Praxismo, Processualismo e Formalismo em Direito Processual Civil. *Genesis: Revista de Direito Processual Civil*, 33.

Mitidiero, D. (2011a). *Colaboração no processo civil: pressupostos sociais, lógicos e éticos* (2nd ed.). Ed. RT.

Mitidiero, D. (2011b). Direito Fundamental ao Processo Justo. *Revista Magister de Direito Civil e Processual Civil*, 45.

Moreira, E. B. (2006). Os princípios constitucionais da atividade econômica. *Revista da Faculdade de Direito da UFPR*, 45.

Mulheron, R. (2004). *The class action in common law legal systems: A comparative perspective*. Hart Publishing.

Muller, A. (2005). *Concepts of culture – Art, politics & society*. University of Calgary Press.

Nagareda, R. (2007). *Mass torts in a world of settlement*. University of Chicago Press.

Netzorg, G. W., & Kern, T. D. (2010). Proportional discovery: Making it the norm, rather than the exception. *Denver University Law Review*, 87.

Nunes, D. J. C. (2008). *Processo jurisdicional democrático: uma análise crítica das reformas processuais*. Juruá.

Offe, C. (1984). Critérios de racionalidade e problemas funcionais da ação político-administrativa. In C. Offe (Ed.), *Problemas Estruturais do Estado Capitalista*. Tempo Brasileiro.

Oliveira, C. A. A. (2003). Poderes do Juiz e Visão Cooperativa do Processo. Genesis. *Revista de Direito Processual Civil*, 27.

Orth, J. V. (2003). *Due process of law – A brief history*. University Press of Kansas.

Osna, G. (2012). Entre a Teoria e a Concretização - Possibilidades, Limites e Funções para uma Nova Lei de Imprensa. *Revista do Instituto dos Advogados do Paraná*, 41.

Osna, G. (2014). *Direitos Individuais Homogêneos: pressupostos, fundamentos e aplicação no processo civil*. Ed. RT.

Pasquino, P. (2001). One and three: Separation of powers and the independence of the judiciary in the Italian constitution. In J. Ferejohn, J. N. Kakove, & J. Riley (Eds.), *Constitutional culture and democratic rule*. Cambridge University Press.

Passos, J. J. C. (2000). *Direito, poder, justiça e processo: julgando os que nos julgam*. Forense.

Posner, R. (1977). *Economic analysis of law* (2nd ed.). Little, Brown and Company.

Posner, R. (1999). *The federal courts – Challenges and reforms*. Harvard University Press.

Posner, R. (2008). *How judges think*. Harvard University Press.

Posner, R. A. (1988). The jurisprudence of skepticism. *Michigan Law Review*, 86.

Posner, R. A. (1990). *The problems of jurisprudence*. Harvard University Press.

Ragone, A. P. (2014). Retrato del revisionismo garantista en el proceso civil a través de Klein y Wach. *Revista de Processo*, 233.

Ragone, A. P. (2016). La revalorización de la audiencia preliminar o preparatoria: una mirada desde la justicia distributiva en el proceso civil. *Revista de Processo*, 252.

Redish, M. (2009). *Wholesale justice – Constitutional democracy and the problem of the class action lawsuit*. Stanford University Press.

Resnik, J. (1995). Many doors? Closing doors? Alternative dispute resolution and adjudication. *Ohio State Journal on Dispute Resolution*, 10.

Rhode, D. L. (2004). *Access to justice*. Oxford University Press.

Ribeiro, S. S. M. (2010). *Direitos Coletivos e Liberdade Individual*. Juruá.

Ripert, G. (1947). *Aspectos jurídicos do capitalismo moderno*. Freitas Bastos.

Roesler, C. R. (2003). Enfoque dogmático e enfoque zetético como pontos de partida para realizar a interdisciplinaridade no Ensino Jurídico Contemporâneo. *Revista Eletrônica de Direito Educacional*, 4.

Roque, A. V. (2013). *Class Action – Ações Coletivas nos Estados Unidos: o que podemos aprender com eles?* Juspodivm.

Rorty, R. (1993). *Contingency, irony and solidarity*. Cambridge University Press.

Rouanet, S. P. (1993). *Mal-estar na modernidade*. Companhia das Letras.

Sacco, R. (2001). *Introdução ao direito comparado*. Ed. RT.

Salamon, L. M., & Anheier, H. K. (1997). *Defining the nonprofit sector: A crossnational analysis*. Manchester University Press.

Sarlet, I. W. (2009). *A eficácia dos direitos fundamentais – uma teoria geral dos direitos fundamentais na perspectiva constitucional* (10th ed.). Livraria do Advogado.

Sarlet, I. W., Marinoni, L. G., & Mitidiero, D. (2012). *Curso de Direito Constitucional*. Ed. RT.

Schauer, F. (2009). *Thinking like a lawyer – A new introduction to legal reasoning*. Harvard University Press.

Scott, J. L. (1998). *Seeing like a state: How certain schemes to improve the human condition have failed*. Yale University Press.

Serbena, C. A. (2010). Objetividade e subjetividade nas ciências jurídicas e sociais: Durkheim e Weber. *Revista da Faculdade de Direito de Uberlândia*, 38.

Shavell, S. (1982). The social versus the private incentive to bring suit in a costly legal system. *The Journal of Legal Studies*, 11.

Silva, O. A. B. (1993). A "Plenitude de Defesa" no Processo Civil. In S. F. Teixeira (Ed.), *As Garantias do Cidadão na Justiça*. Saraiva.

Silva, O. A. B. (2000). *Curso de Processo Civil* (Vol. 1, 5th ed.). Ed. RT.

Silva, O. A. B. (2004). *Processo e Ideologia: o Paradigma Racionalista*. Forense.

Silva, O. A. B., & Gomes, F. (2010). *Teoria Geral do Processo* (5th ed.). Ed. RT.

Silva, V. A. (2002). O proporcional e o razoável. *Revista dos Tribunais*, 798.

Soares, C. H. (2012). Estudo sistemático do direito processual civil chileno. *Revista de Processo*, 223.

Stürner, R., & Kern, C. (2011). Processo civil comparado – Tendências recentes e fundamentais. *Revista de Processo*, 200.

Suarez, C. D. (2013). O panorama atual e a problemática procedimental em torno da tutela inibitória. *Revista de Processo*, 226.

Sundfeld, C. A. (2009). *Fundamentos do Direito Público*. Malheiros.

Sundfeld, C. A. (2012). *Direito Administrativo para Céticos*. Malheiros.

Sunstein, C. R. (2005). *Radical in Robes – Why extreme right-wing courts are wrong for America?* Perseus Books Group.

Talamini, E. (2007). Tutela de Urgência e Fazenda Pública. In C. A. Molinaro, M. G. Milhoranza, & S. G. Porto (Eds.), *Constituição, jurisdição e processo*. Notadez.

Talamini, E. (2015). Arbitragem e a Tutela Provisória no Código de Processo Civil de 2015. *Revista de Arbitragem e Mediação*, 46.

Tamanaha, B. Z. (2009). A concise guide to the rule of law. In G. Palombella & N. Walker (Eds.), *Relocating the rule of law*. Hart Publishing.

Tarello, G. (1989). Quattro buoni giuristi per una cattiva azione. In G. Tarello (Ed.), *Dottrine del processo civile: studi storici sulla formazione del diritto processuale civile*. Il Mulino.

Taruffo, M. (2001). Some remarks on group litigation in comparative perspective. *Duke Journal of Comparative & International Law*, 11.

Taruffo, M. (2009). Cultura e Processo. *Rivista Trimestrale di Diritto e Procedura Civile*, LXIII.

Taruffo, M. (2010). Contro la veriphobia. Osservazioni sparse in risposta a Bruno Cavallone. *Rivista di Diritto Processuale*, 65.

Thompson, J. B. (2003). The theory of structuration. In J. B. Thompson & D. Held (Eds.), *Social theory of modern society: Anthony Giddens and his critics*. Cambridge University Press.

Timm, L. B. (2008). Qual a maneira mais eficiente de prover direitos fundamentais: uma perspectiva de direito e economia? In L. B. Timm & I. W. Sarlet (Eds.), *Direitos Fundamentais: orçamento e reserva do possível*. Livraria do Advogado.

Torrano, B. (2014). *Do fato à legalidade: introdução à teoria analítica do direito*. Lumen Juris.

Trubek, D., & Galanter, M. (1974). Scholars in self-estrangement: Some reflections on the crisis in law and development studies in the United States. *Wisconsin Law Review*, 4.

Trubek, D., & Santos, A. (2006). *The new law and economical development – A critical appraise*. Cambridge University Press.

Tucci, J. R. C. (1990). *Class action e mandado de segurança coletivo, diversificações conceptuais*. Ed. RT.

Uzelac, A. (2012). Goals of civil justice and civil procedure in the contemporary world. In A. Uzelac (Ed.), *Goals of civil justice and civil procedure in contemporary judicial systems*. Springer.

Vasak, K. (1979, July). *For the third generation of human rights: The rights of solidarity*. International Institute of Human Rights.

Venturi, E. (2007). *Processo Civil Coletivo*. Malheiros.

Viehweg, T. (1997). Problemas Sistémicos en la Dogmática Jurídica y en la Investigación Jurídica. In T. Viehweg (Ed.), *Tópica y filosofía del derecho* (2nd ed.). Gedisa.

Violin, J. (2013). *Protagonismo Judiciário e Processo Coletivo Estrutural*. Editora JusPodivm.

Wasserman, R. (2004). *Procedural due process – A reference guide to the American constitution*. Praeger.

Weber, M. (1982). *Ensaios de sociologia*. LTC Editora.

Weber, M. (1989). A "objetividade" do conhecimento nas ciências sociais. In G. Cohn (Ed.), *Max Weber* (3rd ed.). Editora Ática.

Weber, M. (2002). A política como vocação. In H. H. Gerth & C. W. Mills (Eds.), *Ensaios de sociologia*. LTC.

Windscheid, B., & Muther, T. (1974). *Polemica sobre la "actio"*. EJEA.

Yablon, C., & Lansman-Roos, N. (2012). Discovery about discovery: Sampling practice and the resolution of discovery disputes in an age of ever-increasing information. *Cardozo Law Review*, 34.

Zavascki, T. A. (2009). *Antecipação da Tutela* (7th ed.). Saraiva.

Zavascki, T. A. (2014). *Processo Coletivo – Tutela de direitos coletivos e tutela coletiva de direitos* (6th ed.). Ed. RT.

Zuckerman, A. (1996). Lord Woolf's access to justice: Plus a change. *The Modern Law Review*, 59.

MIX
Papier aus verantwortungsvollen Quellen
Paper from responsible sources
FSC® C105338

If you have any concerns about our products,
you can contact us on
ProductSafety@springernature.com

In case Publisher is established outside the EU,
the EU authorized representative is:
Springer Nature Customer Service Center GmbH
Europaplatz 3, 69115 Heidelberg, Germany

Printed by Libri Plureos GmbH
in Hamburg, Germany